C.Krettschmitt

Women Prisoners

WOMEN PRISONERS

A Forgotten Population

Edited by Beverly R. Fletcher,
Lynda Dixon Shaver, and
Dreama G. Moon

Foreword by George Henderson

ILLUSTRATIONS BY LISA J. BILLY

Westport, Connecticut
London

Library of Congress Cataloging-in-Publication Data

Women prisoners : a forgotten population / edited by Beverly R.
  Fletcher, Lynda Dixon Shaver, and Dreama G. Moon ; foreword by
  George Henderson.
       p. cm.
    Includes bibliographical references and index.
    ISBN 0-275-94220-1 (alk. paper)
    1. Women prisoners—United States. I. Fletcher, Beverly R.
  II. Shaver, Lynda Dixon. III. Moon, Dreama G.
  HV9471.W69 1993
  364.3′74′0973—dc20   92-38231

British Library Cataloguing in Publication Data is available.

Library of Congress Catalog Card Number: 92-38231
ISBN: 0-275-94220-1

First published in 1993

Praeger Publishers, 88 Post Road West, Westport, CT 06881
An imprint of Greenwood Publishing Group, Inc.

Printed in the United States of America

The paper used in this book complies with the
Permanent Paper Standard issued by the National
Information Standards Organization (Z39.48-1984).

10 9 8 7 6 5 4 3 2 1

This book is dedicated to the strong and healing spirit of women. This spirit was particularly embodied in the person of Carrie D. Fletcher, a medicine woman, who continues to show us the way.

"Becoming whole again"

Contents

Illustrations

Tables

Figure

Foreword

George Henderson

Perhaps nothing captures the debilitating effects of sexism more vividly than an in-depth study of women incarcerated in our correctional institutions. Beneath the statistics lie a human tragedy of a magnitude most people cannot fully comprehend: a disproportionate number of women are wasting away in nonrehabilitative institutions that perpetuate rather than correct criminal behaviors. The editors and contributors to this book capture cogent slices of life of some of the role players in the prison drama. And they do so with the sensitive touch of social surgeons who carefully lift and examine one layer of human behavior and then another. But they do not stop there. They also examine some of the attitudes, beliefs, and values of incarcerated women and their keepers (prison staff). The total work is an insightful glimpse of a neglected subculture.

Women Prisoners: A Forgotten Population gives new meaning to the phrase "justice delayed is justice denied." The wonderment is not that so many women are imprisoned, but that so few are behind bars. Because of continuing conditions of sexism, I must ask why so few women resort to mayhem. Equally perplexing is why so many women survive their incarceration with even a modicum of sanity. Given the overwhelming negative social, psychological, and environmental conditions characterizing prisons, it is miraculous that most women do indeed survive with their mental faculties intact. The authors point out that it is the social milieu that first drives women to commit crimes and that the same milieu creates government officials who inappropriately punish the offenders. We seem to be a society that must keep our women either pregnant or locked up.

In view of current circumstances, *corrections* does not seem to be a proper term for this process. Belatedly, criminologists are increasingly beginning to believe that the conditions under which most female offenders are handled are a detriment to the correctional ideal of treatment and rehabilitation. Treatment and rehabilitation are the primary functions for only a small proportion of correctional staffs. Instead, three-fourths or more of the nation's correctional personnel are assigned to custody and maintenance functions.

I glean an especially sad note from the authors of this book. Whatever the difference in type and quality among correctional institutions—from large maximum security prisons to open camps without highly visible correctional officers, from short-term detention homes to penitentiaries where women spend most of their lives, from institutions of physical brutality and mentally stultifying routine to those with some rehabilitative programs—there remains an inherent sameness about places where women are imprisoned. They are places where people live apart from their families, with no choice regarding place of residence, selection of intimate associates, or type of occupation—crucial things available in the "free world."

The artificial environment that works against self-reliance and self-control complicates and makes more difficult the reintegration of female offenders into free society. The authors clearly show that sometimes correctional institutions foster conspicuously deleterious conditions such as idleness, corruption, and brutality. A humane penal reform system can be provided only by people with humane intentions. One of the greatest current wastes, and one which the authors implicitly encourage us to avoid in the future, is that of human resources. Without immediate attention to salvaging our female prisoner resources as well as their children, our nation will become victims of its own neglect and abuse.

If we take no action concerning women in prison, the negative consequences for the future could be staggering. No doubt it would be impressive to have available quantitative data for the societal costs and consequences over the decades ahead that will result if we maintain the present faltering correctional system. Unfortunately, it is impossible to provide such data with the same accuracy as voter opinion polls. Fortunately, the ineffectiveness of the current system is no longer a subject of controversy. Enlightened persons, including those within the penal system, acknowledge the necessity of positive change.

It is not enough to merely "see" women in prison. In the end, the best strategy is to provide them with opportunities to earn decent wages, eat wholesome diets, nurture loved ones in happy families, live in safe environments, and die timely deaths unhurried by sexism. No, female inmates do not need separate but equal penal facilities. On the contrary, they need equal opportunities to live in a free world. The authors of this book provide data that can be helpful in recreating the lives of women offenders. The question is, Who will now take action to make our penal institutions places of healing rather than destruction?

Preface

The Project for Recidivism Research and Female Inmate Training (PRRFIT), a multidisciplinary, multiethnic applied research project, was created in early 1990. Its purpose is to conduct a longitudinal study of the *individual* and *institutional* factors that promote recidivism among female offenders and ultimately intervene in the cycle of recidivism. We have elected to study current female inmates in order to capture the effects of various institutional factors on recidivism.

Because previous research has failed to address the problems of imprisoned women from a holistic point of view, two unique features of this project are recognition of the importance of women researching women, and its multidisciplinary and multiethnic approach. We started this project with three coprincipal investigators: Beverly R. Fletcher, an African American: Dreama G. Moon, an Anglo: and Lynda Dixon Shaver, a Cherokee woman. The project team has grown to include both women and men. We are professors, graduate students, and undergraduates in the fields of sociology, psychology, anthropology, English, communication, social work, and human relations at the University of Oklahoma. We are composed of African Americans, Native Americans, Caucasians, and Asians. PRRFIT research is being conducted in collaboration with the Oklahoma Department of Corrections.

OVERALL PROJECT DESIGN

The state of Oklahoma is an important place in which to conduct our research. It was chosen as the research site because it has the highest per capita rate of female incarceration in the nation. Data from the Oklahoma

Department of Corrections *Female Offender Task Force Report* (1989) indicate that the number of women residents in Oklahoma correction centers is increasing at an alarming pace and has been accompanied by unprecedented rates of recidivism.

Although our subject populations, inmates and staff at Oklahoma correctional facilities for women, pose challenges (e.g., access, confidentiality, sampling, and research administration) for social science researchers, they are populations that need to be studied, particularly from the point of view of the female offender. We use survey methodology, in-depth interviews, and field observations in our research. In short, we employ methodological triangulation in an attempt to build upon the strengths of different methods. Using survey methodology gives us generalizability across our incarcerated population, in-depth interviews allow for validity cross-checks, and field observations provide depth of meaning to the data.

Table P.1 is an outline of the activities of the project.

As shown in Table P.1, "PRRFIT Research Design," the project consists of program design, implementation, and evaluation as well as data gath-

Table P.1	
PRRFIT Research Design	
	Projected Timeline
LITERATURE REVIEW	Dec. 31, 1991, ongoing*
SURVEYS	
Inmate survey design	Mar. 31, 1991
Staff** survey design	Mar. 31, 1991
Inmate survey administration	Dec. 31, 1991
Staff survey administration	Dec. 31, 1991
Inmate survey data analysis	May 31, 1993
Staff survey data analysis	May 31, 1993
IN-DEPTH INTERVIEWS	
Inmates	Sep. 30, 1993
Staff	Nov. 30, 1993
Inmate interview data analysis	Feb. 28, 1994
Staff interview data analysis	Apr. 30, 1994
FIELD OBSERVATIONS	
Observations of inmates and staff, together and apart during survey administration and interviews	Nov. 30, 1993
Observation data analysis	Dec. 31, 1993
PROGRAMS (development, design, implementation, evaluation)	Dec. 31, 1993, ongoing
* "Ongoing" means that although there is a specified deadline, it is anticipated that this process will continue indefinitely.	
** "Staff" refers to administration, staff, line, and support personnel at Oklahoma Correctional Centers for women.	

ering and analysis. As a long-term research project, PRRFIT requires the efforts of many individuals from a variety of disciplines. This study is an important step in examining factors associated with the rising rates of female recidivism. Moreover, this timely research will provide a data base that will ultimately lead to the development and institutionalization of strategies to interrupt the cycle of female inmate recidivism in Oklahoma.

Surveys of Inmates and Staff

In 1991, in collaboration with the Oklahoma Department of Corrections, inmate and staff surveys were administered at two primary prison facilities for women in the state of Oklahoma, which we shall refer to in this book as Site 1 and Site 2.

Inmates in these facilities represent over 90 percent of all incarcerated women in the state of Oklahoma. This book reports inmate findings from data collected at Site 1 and staff findings from data collected at both Sites 1 and 2. Inmate survey data from Site 2 are currently being analyzed.

Both the inmate and the staff surveys were developed by the PRRFIT research team in conjunction with the Research and Planning Division of the Oklahoma Department of Corrections. Researchers were present while surveys were being completed in order to answer questions and to assist prisoners who were illiterate or semiliterate or who spoke another language as their first language. In addition, PRRFIT researchers made field observations during inmate and staff orientations and during the survey administrations.

The inmate survey administered at Site 1 consisted of 142 questions, both closed and open-ended. Some of the questions were Likert scaled, others required inmates to circle the appropriate response, and some required write-in responses. A variety of questions were asked, including questions that would provide a demographic profile of the women. The survey specifically inquired about family, economic status, sexual orientation, self-image, criminal history, history of abuse, alcohol and drug usage, treatment history, health, and program needs. The inmate survey administered at Site 2 contained the original 142 questions asked at Site 1 plus 20 additional questions about self-concept, support systems, and spirituality.

Two pilot tests were conducted on the original inmate survey to ensure that the questions were clearly written and unbiased and that they solicited the information being sought. The first pilot test was administered to three subjects who were on parole and had a history of recidivism. A second pilot test was conducted with 20 inmates at Site 1. Revisions to the survey were made based on the feedback received from these pilot studies.

The staff survey administered at the two research sites consisted of 113 questions. The survey asked about family, economic status, self-image, job satisfaction, inmate and staff program needs, perceptions about female prisoners, and information to be used in compiling a staff demographic profile.

Site 1 is the only maximum security facility in Oklahoma. It houses maximum (including death row), medium, and minimum security female prisoners. It has an average daily population of over 300 inmates; the population was 325 inmates at the time the survey was administered.

The researchers administered surveys to 279 inmates (Table P.2). Usable responses were received from a total of 267 inmates, or 82 percent of the inmate population at Site 1. This represents approximately 40 percent of the entire population of women inmates in the state of Oklahoma.

The sample from Site 1 is significant. The results from this survey provide a number of insights and generalizations about the population of women prisoners in the state of Oklahoma.

Field Observations

Field observations were conducted by PRRFIT team members during the survey portion of our assessment at both Site 1 and Site 2, and similar observations will be made during the interview phase of our assessment.

Some PRRFIT team members underwent training in field observation from a professor in the Anthropology Department at the University of Oklahoma. Team members were given the opportunity to discuss and practice field observation techniques through role playing and were asked

Table P.2		
Research Samples		
Inmate Research Sample	Site 1	Site 2
Total female inmate population	325	346
Total usable surveys	267	290
Sample as a percent of population	82.1%	83.8%
Staff Research Sample	Site 1	Site 2
Total staff population	125	131
Total usable surveys	68	95
Sample as a percent of population	54.4%	72.5%

to evaluate their own performance. They were also given an observation guide to incorporate into their field experience and encouraged to make detailed field notes of the sites, including rough maps of the areas where the surveys were conducted. Other team members were experienced in ethnographic field observation methods.

In both of the women's prisons, the surveys were given in areas such as dining rooms, conference rooms, and inmates' dorms or cells. They also were administered to death row inmates at Site 1. PRRFIT team members were given access to all of these areas during the time the women were completing the surveys, and freely mingled with both inmates and correctional staff. This provided an opportunity for field observations of the physical settings, inmate and staff appearance, the behavior and interactions of inmates and staff with each other, and their interaction with PRRFIT team members. These field observations helped us to make sense of much of our data.

Interviews of Inmates and Staff

One important advantage of the interview process is the opportunity it provides for face-to-face contact between researchers and their subjects. The primary benefit, however, is that interviews serve as a reliability and validity check for both survey and observational data. By being on the scene, the interviewer can clear up any misunderstandings as well as give respondents the opportunity to give in-depth information in certain areas.

In the interview, the researcher has the opportunity to do more extensive field observations, noting not only verbal responses but the interviewees' nonverbal behavior and the environmental impact. While some preliminary interviews have already been conducted at Site 1, we have projected the completion of inmate and staff interviews at Sites 1 and 2 by November 1993. An Interview Guide for this part of our assessment has been prepared by members of the PRRFIT team.

The Literature Review

Our research would not be complete without a thorough review of past research studies and other existing literature on the topic of incarcerated women. PRRFIT has conducted an extensive literature search and review and continues to look for relevant literature. Each chapter contains references to relevant literature on the subject matter discussed in the chapter.

Reliability and Validity

Reliability can be thought of as the degree to which observed scores are free from measurement error (Dooley, 1990). In other words, reliability is concerned with measurement theory, that is, separating out how much a score reflects its "true" value and how much of it is composed of error due to measurement. Reliability can be increased by standardization, that is, by making sure that identical instructions and procedures are followed to elicit measures of the same construct. In our research we do this by ensuring that researchers are trained in common procedures and that the surveys are administered to respondents in as similar a manner as possible in the same environments.

Validity refers to the inferences made from measurement, or the "fit between the measure and label" (Dooley, 1990, p. 82). Validity is concerned with whether a measure does indeed measure what it purports to measure. It is axiomatic that in order to be valid a measure must be reliable. However, reliability does not guarantee that a measure is valid. In short, a measure may correctly tap an underlying construct, but it may be the "wrong" construct. Given this shortcoming, high validity is to be strived for since it entails both high reliability and a close fit between measure and construct (Rolison, 1992).

Threats to validity in survey research stem from the tendency of some people to respond positively to any set of questions and the tendency of others to present themselves in the most favorable light possible. The first of these is often referred to as "yea saying," while the second is typically known as social desirability bias. We have attempted to control for both of these threats to validity in our survey and question design. For this reason, items are ordered both positively and negatively in terms of response category, and neutral wording is used when possible.

Validity is typically measured in three general categories: (1) criterion validity, (2) content validity, and (3) construct validity. Criterion validity attempts to assess validity by comparing the level of association of a study's measure with an already validated measure of the same underlying construct. Unfortunately, for many of our measures, criteria are not available. Given the absence of validated measures for other constructs of interest in our study, we often rely upon content validity, that is, our appraisal of whether our measures tap the domain of our underlying construct. Finally, we use construct validity to test whether our items measure the intended underlying construct. To do this, we rely most often on factor analysis to see whether our measures do indeed highly correlate with each other on the intended construct more than they do on other constructs. At a broader level, we control for method effects by employing a multimethod technique in the design of the study (Dooley, 1990). In particular, to control for error, we supplement our survey methodology with in-depth interviewing and field observation.

Acknowledgments

There are always more people than the authors involved in creating a book. First and foremost, we would like to acknowledge and thank the imprisoned women in Oklahoma for completing our surveys, despite the many inconveniences involved, and for talking to team members at great length during unexpected times and in unusual places about their personal experiences. Without their unique contributions, this research would not have been possible. The staffs of the women's maximum and minimum security prisons in Oklahoma have our deepest appreciation for their cooperation in completing our lengthy staff survey and their willingness to assist and dialogue with us.

To Ruby, Garry, Kathleen, Regina, Debbie, Vivian, Connie, Susan, Paula, Elizabeth, and Yu, the researchers and authors responsible for individual chapters in this book, to Lisa for the illustrations, and to the other researchers on our team, Heidi Hartman, Phyllis Nabilsi, and Michele Parker, we express immeasurable gratitude. By donating countless hours of personal time and effort in collecting, inputting, and analyzing data and shaping the information into chapters, they have demonstrated belief in the need for this type of ongoing research about women in prison. Collectively and as individuals, their ideas, insights, support, and constructive criticisms have been invaluable.

We especially thank Kathleen A. O'Shea for a superb job in completing the tedious task of indexing this book. We thank Professor Betty Harris for providing training in field observations and interviewing techniques. Thanks to Bob Shull and Chong Ho Yu for computer programming consultation, Sushil Rungta for putting in endless hours of data, and Kathryn Adkins for proofreading. We acknowledge Michelle D. Parker for her critiques, Bonnie and Ron Cox for their computer time, and Betty Jo Dowler, teacher, mother, and fan club.

Our thanks go to Dr. George Henderson, chair of the Department of Human Relations, University of Oklahoma, for his support and for writing the foreword to this book, and to his office staff for assistance with numerous and varied requests. We also thank Susan B. Loving, attorney general of Oklahoma, for her endorsements, and Dr. Daniel J. O'Neil, vice president of Research at the University of Oklahoma, for providing the means by which our team could travel to the Academy of Criminal Justice Sciences Conference in Pittsburgh to present our research. We express our thanks to the Southwest Regional Center for Drug-Free Schools and Communities, in particular Anita Fream, associate director, and Shiva Fazlalizadeh, for copy services and personnel assistance.

And finally, we thank the Oklahoma Department of Corrections for assistance with this ongoing research project. In particular, we thank Mr. Gary Maynard, director of the Oklahoma Department of Corrections, as well as Mr. David Miller and Mr. Larry Fields, deputy directors. To Warden Howard Ray, Warden Joy Hadwiger, Warden Neville Massie, Deputy Warden Richard Morton, Deputy Warden Gregg Williams, and Mr. Phillip Garland, assistant to the warden, we extend a special thanks.

Women Prisoners

ONE   *The Population*

In Part One we meet the female offender as she is today. We look at who she is, how she thinks and feels, her experiences and ethnic origins, her life, and even her death.

Each of the chapters in Part One focuses on a specific aspect of the literature and on project data analyses. Chapter 1, by Beverly R. Fletcher and Dreama G. Moon, is an introduction to the book that highlights the significance of studying imprisoned women, discusses recidivism, and presents a historical perspective on the study of female criminality.

In Chapter 2, "The Woman Prisoner," Beverly R. Fletcher, Garry L. Rolison, and Dreama G. Moon profile the woman offender and give an overview of important findings that serve as stepping stones for in-depth exploration by other authors in the book.

Constance Hardesty, Paula G. Hardwick, and Ruby J. Thompson take a look at how self-esteem influences the lives of women offenders in Chapter 3, "Self Esteem and the Woman Prisoner."

Chapter 4, "Patterns of Substance Use among Women in Prison," by Dreama G. Moon, Ruby J. Thompson, and Regina Bennett, provides important information about the relationship of drug use to crime and also draws some specific conclusions from our research data about the impact of drug use on the life of an offender.

"Abuse and the Woman Prisoner" is examined closely in Chapter 5 by Elizabeth Sargent, Susan Marcus-Mendoza, and Chong Ho Yu. They examine the effects of childhood abuse and abuse as adults on women in prison. They also discuss important correlations between abuse and other variables.

In Chapter 6, "African American Women in Prison," by Deborah Brinkley-Jackson, Vivian L. Carter, and Garry L. Rolison, some significant differences between women of color and white women inmates are illuminated.

Chapter 7, "Women on Death Row," by Kathleen A. O'Shea, concludes this section with information about the most forgotten of the forgotten population: the women on death row. She looks at capital punishment and how the court system in this country has meted out the death penalty to women.

"Screaming to be heard"

1 Introduction

Beverly R. Fletcher and Dreama G. Moon

Untitled Poem

I wake in the middle-of-the-night terror
alone in the conviction that I am in a prison cell
shut away, suddenly, from all that makes my life
I sense the great weight of the prison
pressing down on the little box of room I lie in
alone   forgotten.

How often do women awake
in the prison of marriage
of solitary motherhood,
alone and forgotten.
Of exhaustion from meaningless work,
of self-despising learned early,
of advancing age,
alone and forgotten.

How many women lie awake at this moment
struggling as I do against despair
knowing the morning will crush us once again
under the futility of our lives?
And how short a step it is for us
to the more obvious imprisonment
of bars and concrete
where our sisters lie
alone   forgotten.

See now, in this middle-of-the-night emptiness
how little it matters

> whether we wear a convict's ill-made cotton dress
> or a velvet pantsuit.
> We are possessions to be bought and sold
> we are children to be curbed and patronized
> we are bodies to be coveted, seized, and rejected
> when our breasts begin to sag
> we are dummies to be laughed at.
> I sense the great weight of the society
> pressing down on the little box of a room I lie in
> alone   and forgotten.

Untitled poem by Erika Huggins (1982)
Reprinted with permission from *Off Our Backs*, 2 (8), Washington, D.C.

In this chapter, we take a look at the literature relevant to women in prison, explore the concept of recidivism and how it is measured, and examine the ways in which traditional criminological theory has approached the study of female criminality and its impact on women in prison.

THE SIGNIFICANCE OF STUDYING A FORGOTTEN POPULATION

A scarcity of literature about women offenders indicates that crime by women has yet to be thoroughly studied. Lee H. Bowker (1978) noted this gap over a decade ago:

It would be easier to study a woman's prison than a male facility since the smaller size of women's institutions makes the task of data collection much more manageable than it could ever be in the massive male structures that dot every state in the union. Despite this fact, the literature of female correctional subcultures is quite limited. There are a number of factors that have contributed to this, among which are (1) only four percent of American prisoners are women [this percentage is now 5.7%], (2) women are generally thought of as being less criminal than men, (3) most graduate school professors, grant-awarding panel members, and other powerful administrators are male, and (4) almost all correctional scientists are male. Considering the cultural and structural forces arrayed against concentrating research resources on the study of incarcerated females, we are lucky to know as much as we do about the topic. (p. 43)

Bowker's view is still relevant today. Although the female inmate population continues to grow at a rate far greater than that of males, we still know very little about female criminality (Fletcher, Shaver, and Moon, 1991). Nationally, between 1980 and 1989, the number of women prisoners increased by 202 percent, compared to a 112 percent increase for males

(Bureau of Justice Statistics, 1991f). As of 1989, women comprised 5.7 percent of the total prison population in the United States—the highest number since statistical collection was started in 1926 (Bureau of Justice Statistics, 1991f).

Little research on women's recidivism has been done. For the most part, studies on recidivism have been conducted on all-male groups or mixed gender groups having a small female sampling. These studies indicate that recidivism rates in general are very high. For example, one study found that a third of the released offenders in fourteen states returned to prison within three years (Bureau of Justice Statistics, 1987). A recent Bureau of Justice Statistics report (1991f) found that over two-thirds of the women in prison in 1986 were recidivists. The paucity of knowledge about female recidivism demonstrates a compelling need for more research.

Although women represent only 5.7 percent of the total prison population in the United States, they make up 8.6 percent of Oklahoma's prison population (Bureau of Justice Statistics, 1991e). For the past two years, Oklahoma has incarcerated more women per capita than any other state in the country. A report by the Oklahoma Department of Corrections (1991) indicates that in 1990, female recidivists comprised 19.6 percent of all women in prison—a 9.7 percent increase since 1980. According to our data (Project For Recidivism Research and Female Inmate Training, 1991), the numbers are much higher than previously thought; 46 percent of our sample has been previously imprisoned at least once. Numbers clearly indicate that Oklahoma is a crucial location in which to conduct research on women recidivists.

RECIDIVISM

The concept of recidivism is a complex one to measure. Recidivism has been—and is currently—defined in various ways by lay people, corrections professionals, and academicians. To some, offenders can be said to become recidivists when they are returned to prison; to others, offenders are called recidivists when they happen to be rearrested whether ultimately convicted or not. To the layperson, recidivism occurs when the former offender "does it" again. Some statistics include juvenile arrests and/or convictions as part of their determination as to whether offenders can be labeled recidivists, while other statistics do not. These various conceptualizations of recidivism make the researcher's task extremely complicated, as researchers are not necessarily talking about the same thing when discussing recidivism. In essence, researchers create higher or lower recidivism rates by the way they choose to define recidivism. Unfortunately, this problem is not one that can be rectified in the context of this book. What we as responsible scholars are obligated to do is provide the reader with our own working definition of recidivism as well as the reasons we have chosen this conceptualization over other competing definitions. In order to do so, we examine various definitions of recidivism that appear in the literature and the reasoning behind these various interpretations and then present our definition.

To the layperson, a very clear and concise way of thinking about recidivism is to define it as a tendency to slip back into a previous, especially criminal, pattern of behavior. The confusion starts when criminal justice practitioners and theorists attempt to pinpoint exactly when the "slip" occurs. Is it at rearrest, upon reconviction, or on the offender's return to prison? The Bureau of Justice Statistics (1988a) measures recidivism in three ways: rearrest, reconviction, and reincarceration. In some studies, the Bureau of Justice Statistics includes prior juvenile probation and/or conviction records, as they do, for example, in the *Special Report: Women in Prison* (Bureau of Justice Statistics, 1991f); in other studies they do not include juvenile history (see for example, Bureau of Justice Statistics, 1989b, *Recidivism of Prisoners Released in 1983*). Some researchers find including rearrests in a measure of recidivism to be problematic. For instance, Martin, Cloniger, and Guze (1978) maintain that reconviction and return to prison are more reliable indicators of recidivism because they conclude that arrest rates are influenced by a number of factors, including police vigilance or harassment, the neighborhood in which one lives, and the race of the arrestee. Since theoretically innocence is assumed until guilt has been established, arrest may not be a practical measure of recidivism. Others disagree with this position. For example, the U.S. President's Commission on Law Enforcement and Administration of Justice measures recidivism at the point of arrest (U.S. National Commission on the Causes and Prevention of Violence, 1971). Although studies using this measurement include a number of people arrested for crimes they did not commit, this number compensates for those freed for legal or technical reasons even though it is believed that they did commit the crime.

For the purposes of this book, we use the most conservative definition of recidivism, which is the return to prison for either the commission of a new crime or a rule violation. We choose this measure over others for two reasons: (1) our main focus is on women's prison experience, and (2) we believe that return to prison is a practical and clear-cut measure of recidivism.

A HISTORICAL PERSPECTIVE ON THE STUDY OF
FEMALE CRIMINALITY

The academic discipline that informs the decision making and policy formation of crime control agencies such as prisons is criminal justice (Newman, 1975). In turn, criminal justice is informed by a number of disciplines, most notably criminology, political science, and law. Criminological theory has the greatest impact on criminal justice (Moon, 1990).

Criminology is usually a subconcentration in a sociology or psychology curriculum (Newman, 1975). It is primarily concerned with crime causation, whereas criminal justice addresses the degree of effectiveness of intervention into criminal matters. The interrelationship of the two disciplines is described by Newman (1975): "The effectiveness or dysfunction of criminal justice intervention may be tested against, and in turn test, hypotheses and theories of crime causation proposed by criminologists" (p. x).

Theories about crime causation (i.e., criminological theory) have impacted the study of women. Historically, criminology has been concerned with the activities and interests of men. Criminological theory addresses women and crime by generalizing from what is known about male crime. Morris (1987) states:

Theories of criminality have been developed from male subjects and validated on male subjects. Thus they are "man made." There is nothing wrong with this per se, but the theories have tended to be generalized to all criminals. . . . It is assumed that the theories will apply to women; many do not. . . . Relying on male subjects or on men's experience has two implications. It means that, first, these theories are really special theories about *men's crime* and secondly, that doubts must arise about a particular theory's validity as a general theory if it does not apply to women. (p. 2)

Criticisms directed against criminology carry two main themes: "the remarkable, indeed perverse, exclusion of females from consideration in criminological literature and the distortion of the experiences of women offenders to fit certain inappropriate stereotypes" (Heidensohn, 1985, p. 146).

Historically, researchers and writers in the field of criminology have seen criminality as the result of individual characteristics that are only peripherally affected by economic, social, and political forces. These characteristics are of a physiological and psychological nature and are based on implicit and explicit assumptions about the inherent nature of women. This nature is seen as universal rather than existing within a

specific historical framework (Klein, 1982). Due to this focus, two distinct classes of women have been created: (1) "good girls" who are not criminals and (2) "bad girls" who are criminals. Klein states that this moral position has often masqueraded as scientific distinction. This focus on the individual as causation has led theorists to prescribe various remedies for female criminality, ranging from sterilization to psychoanalysis. The focus on individual adjustment has laid the groundwork for the traditional model of rehabilitation, that is: "She is broken; let's fix her and make her a good girl."

It is important to briefly review the theories that continue to impact our notions about female criminality today. In 1903, Lombroso, whose work has been effectively discredited, described female criminality as an inherent, biological tendency (Klein, 1982). If these biological defects were not allowed to breed, crime would eventually disappear. This fascination with physiological causation has not disappeared.

Both Thomas and Freud extended the physiological concept of criminality to include psychological factors. Klein (1982) states:

It is critical to understand that these psychological notions are based on assumptions of universal *physiological* traits of women, such as their reproductive instinct and passivity. . . . Women may be viewed as turning to crime as a *perversion* of or *rebellion against* their *natural feminine roles*. Whether their problems are biological, psychological, or social environmental, the point is always to return them to their roles. (p. 37; emphasis added)

Other criminological theorists cited by Heidensohn (1985), such as Pollack and Davis, focus on female sexuality and stereotypical notions about women in general. One recurring theme explains economic crimes like prostitution using sexual interpretations—"bad girls" again. The theory of women as hidden criminals proposes the following: (1) that women are innately deceitful and therefore better at concealing crime than men and (2) that they probably manipulate men into committing crimes with their "wily ways." Criminologists who use these theories make two key unquestioned assumptions about women: first, they assume a universal female nature free of culture, class, and historical considerations, and second, they emphasize sexual factors in the causation of female crime to the exclusion of economic and social factors (Heidensohn, 1985). Klein (1982) maintains that "to do a new kind of research on women and crime . . . it is necessary to understand the assumptions made by the traditional writers and to break away from them" (p. 58). Klein proposes that research into the causation of female criminality must be conducted within a social and economic context.

Smart (as cited in Heidensohn, 1985) provides a full-scale critique of conventional criminology. She systematically maps the nature of female criminality, assesses the contributions of noted criminologists to studies of female crime, and calls for more research on women and crime. Leonard (1982) extends the critique into new territory by examining the major criminological theories of anomie, labeling, differential association, delinquent subcultures, and critical criminology. She concludes that while two of these traditional theories, labeling and critical criminology, offer potentially valuable and undeveloped insights into women and crime, the remaining conceptualizations offer no understanding relevant to the causation of female crime.

Increases in the female crime rate have been linked to the emancipation of women for more than a century. A controversial debate has developed that is one of the few aspects of women and crime to have sparked broad interest, both among academics and in the popular media. In studies cited by Heidensohn (1985), Simon concludes that the emancipation of women means harsher treatment of women by crime control agencies. On the other hand, Adler (1975) argues that emancipation is linked to the rise in female crime. Smart (as cited in Heidensohn, 1985) argues that rises in female crime are not new phenomena and that socioeconomic factors have to be considered when examining such increases. Box and Hale (as cited in Heidensohn, 1985) maintain:

The new female criminal is more a social invention than an empirical reality and the proposed relationship between the women's movement and crime is indeed tenuous and even vacuous. Women are still typically non-violent, petty property offenders. (p. 158)

Chesney-Lind (as cited in Heidensohn, 1985) sees a sinister design behind the moral panic over the new, aggressive female criminals, and she states that "the invention of the liberated female crook forced the female offender to bear the brunt of the hostility towards the women's movement" (p. 160). She maintains that this "invention" serves the purpose of providing "facts" that point to the "dark" side of emancipation and that it distracts attention from the real problems in the criminal justice system. For better or worse, this debate has served to make female crime more visible.

Today, women are still often invisible in conventional studies of criminology. A few criminologists, however, have taken a new approach to the study of women and crime. Most notably, Box and Harris (as cited in

Heidensohn, 1985) have incorporated women and gender variables into their research and have criticized others for failure to do so. A new strain of criminology is developing that demands new ways of studying women and crime (Heidensohn, 1985).

The development of criminological theory that will truly impact the daily reality of the lives of women in prison from the policy-making level down is still in the future. Prisons for women still operate according to the conventional "wisdom" and practices of traditional criminological and criminal justice theory. The purpose of penal systems clearly is to deal with male crime; female criminals and their needs are simply squeezed into this model. At best, it is an uncomfortable fit. Although programs for women in prison may look different on the surface than they did ten years ago, one has only to examine underlying assumptions to uncover traditional criminological thought and practice. When looking at programs for women in prison, some basic questions should be asked: What view of women do these programs assume? How do program opportunities for women inmates compare to those of their male counterparts?

Paradoxically, women's "underachievement" in committing crimes does not bring them benefits in the prison system. Although women comprise only 5.7 percent of the total prison population in this country compared to their male counterparts, they are "rewarded" with the most inadequate and remotely located facilities, fewer opportunities for vocational and educational programs, inadequate or no health and medical care, fewer work assignments, lower pay for the same jobs performed by male inmates, a greater use of tranquilizers and psychotropic medications as a means of social control, and greater loss of parental rights (Mann, 1984). According to Moon (1990), reasons typically given to explain these deficits are: (1) the small number of female inmates makes the cost of better services prohibitive (does this mean that if more women committed crimes, female prisoners would benefit?), (2) women offenders are not dangerous, so there is no need to spend a lot of money on rehabilitation (if more women were dangerous, would female prisoners benefit?), and (3) women prisoners are not demanding—that is, they are not as likely to riot over poor conditions as are men inmates (does this mean that if women became more violent, female prisoners would benefit?).

Female inmates are punished twofold because they do not commit crimes at the same rate as men, because they mainly commit "nice" crimes like theft and check fraud, and because they do not generally use violent means to get what they need. Prison, like society in general, sends a real double message to females in prison. (Moon, 1990, p. 10)

The quantity of available programs is problematic, as is the quality of that programming. For example, in a study cited by Ross and Fabiano (1986), Haft finds that vocational training programs for women in prison provide skills that are not in demand in the outside job market and do not provide a livable wage. In institutions that provide vocational training, it is almost always limited to stereotypical female jobs like domestic work, hairdressing, typing, sewing, and nurse's aide work. Ross and Fabiano (1986) find that

the primary goal of programs for female prisoners is often teaching "femininity"—how to walk, talk, and carry themselves. This is related both to the view that female offenders have "failed" as women and must be retrained for the role; and the view that the only hope for women prisoners is marriage. (p. 29)

It is apparent that the numbers of women returning to prison are consistently increasing each year. This trend will probably continue unless the needs and problems of women inmates are adequately addressed. It is imperative that theories of criminality be developed that take into account the realities of female offenders' lives, including the similarities and real differences that exist between female and male offenders. These theories must not be based on sexist notions of femininity or of "women's nature," but instead must incorporate the concept of women's oppression as well as the special challenges related to female criminality that women face in our society. We must also offer analyses of the effects of special characteristics such as race and class as experienced by women offenders. Furthermore, the close scrutiny of prisons for women is needed desperately if we are to effectively intervene in the cycle of recidivism experienced by women prisoners. All facets of female prison institutions must be reevaluated in light of what we now know about the needs of women in prison, and appropriate changes must be made. The remainder of this book will provide insights and information that may serve as a starting place for the reevaluation and restructuring of prisons for women.

2   The Woman Prisoner

Beverly R. Fletcher, Garry L. Rolison, and Dreama G. Moon

This chapter presents an overview of preliminary findings, submits questions for research, and makes comparisons between our sample of women inmates from Site 1 with men and women imprisoned throughout the United States. Making such comparisons is fraught with problems. For example, information on some indicators is available for women but not for men. Additionally, sources sometimes present data in unaggregated form and sometimes in aggregated form for each population. Furthermore, different data sources sometimes disagree with each other. Added to this comparability problem has been an evident gender bias that differentially records information for men and women inmates. In short, it has been difficult to develop comparable data for each group. Despite these difficulties, it is important to place our sample of women from Site 1 in some comparative context so that their relative degree of representativeness can be assessed.

A NATIONAL PROFILE OF THE WOMAN PRISONER

In 1990 the American Correctional Association published a profile of the adult female inmate. The following summarizes the results of the study.

Personal History

The typical adult female inmate is a woman of color between the ages of 25 and 29 who is a single parent and has never been married. She has one to three children who are being cared for by her mother or grandparent during her incarceration. When she is released, she plans to live with her parents or grandparents and maintain custody of her children.

Home Life

She is a product of a single-parent home. She indicates that her children and her mother are the most important people in her life. As a minor she ran away from home one to three times due to feelings of insecurity about parental acceptance and love, and she is easily manipulated by her peers. Fifty percent of imprisoned women have other family members who have been incarcerated, of which 54 percent are their siblings.

Physical Abuse

Between the ages of 5 and 14, the typical female prisoner was the victim of sexual abuse. She was more than likely sexually abused by a male member of her immediate family, usually her father or stepfather. If she reported the incident to someone, it resulted in no change in the abuser's behavior or it made matters worse.

Alcohol/Drug History

By the time she was 13 or 14 years old she started using drugs and/or alcohol. Before her incarceration, she used alcohol no less than one or two times a month and she used cocaine, speed, and marijuana on a daily basis. She abuses drugs to make herself feel better emotionally, and she has most likely attempted suicide because of depression, believing that life is too painful and that nobody cares.

Treatment Programs

The typical woman inmate reports that she would participate in programs that would help or assist her if they were available. She indicates that the most helpful programs are drug and alcohol treatment programs and job training.

Educational Background

The typical woman prisoner dropped out of high school, and 34 percent of the dropouts failed to graduate because of pregnancy. Forty-nine percent attended vocational school as adults, studying to be secretaries, medical assistants, dental assistants, or cosmetologists.

Work History

The typical woman inmate has previous experience as a clerk or in the areas of sales and services. Fifty-four percent of the women have held an average of one to three jobs a year before their imprisonment, with their highest wages ranging from $3.36 to $6.50 an hour. Sixty percent received welfare assistance before incarceration, and 65 percent say that they are qualified to perform either service-oriented or clerical jobs. About 11 percent of the women have received some vocational training in prison, and 81 percent state that they want and need more education and experience in order to obtain jobs when they are released.

Criminal History

The typical female prisoner has been arrested two to nine times starting at the age of 15, and her most common offenses are property crimes and crimes of violence. Her current sentence is two to eight years, and she will serve approximately one-fourth of her sentence. Her crimes were committed to relieve economic pressures, to pay for drugs, or because of poor judgment, and she reacted to her first incarceration with fear, disbelief, or resignation.

Program Benefits

She indicates that educational programs would be the most helpful to her, followed by substance abuse programs and church programs.

The description given depicts the typical (or "average") woman prisoner in the United States. These characterizations based on averages may portray an unrealistic picture, as they do not encompass the variety of women in prison. Although they are useful for descriptions, averages create a stereotype of the female inmate, and the danger is in developing programs for the "typical" woman in prison and not meeting the needs of most women prisoners. This book sketches a profile that includes averages but also attempts to capture the wide range of diversity among women in prison.

A PROFILE OF THE WOMAN PRISONER IN OKLAHOMA

Oklahoma leads the nation in the proportion of inmates who are women. Almost 1 out of 11 (8.6%) of all Oklahoma inmates are women, as compared to the national average of nearly 1 out of 18 (5.7%) (Bureau of Justice Statistics, 1991e). This fact alone makes Oklahoma an important site in which to study female offenders.

The average age of women in our sample is 32.3 years. Slightly more than one-quarter (27.4%) are married. More than 6 out of 10 have completed either a GED or have a high school diploma (64.1%). These women are evenly divided between being holders of the GED (32%) and holders of a high school diploma (32%). Most of Oklahoma's inmates come from the state of Oklahoma (60%). Fifty-two percent are women of color and 48 percent are white. The category "women of color" includes African Americans, Native Americans, and Hispanic women. Although African Americans comprise approximately 7 percent of the population in Oklahoma, 37 percent of our sample at Site 1 is African American. First arrest of Oklahoma's average female inmate occurs at age 22, and the first incarceration at age 26. Slightly more than a quarter (26.6%) have been incarcerated as juveniles. As adults they have been arrested for misdemeanors on an average of 2.1 times and for felonies an average of 3.1 times. Over half (53.9%) are imprisoned for the first time, and 46.1% have been incarcerated more than once as an adult. Over 95 percent of our sample are mothers.

COMPARISONS

Comparing Oklahoma's women prisoners to a nationwide profile of women inmates reveals some differences we discuss next.

Table 2.1 displays the data for our sample and the national population of female and male inmates on selected indicators. Striking differences between our sample of women inmates at Site 1 and the national profile occur with respect to age, racial demographics, the relatively high rates of marriage and motherhood, the relatively high rats of physical and sexual abuse reported, the relatively lower rates of drug use, the higher level of educational attainment, the higher age at first arrest and imprisonment, the relatively low proportion of violent offenders, and the relatively high proportion of drug offenders. Each of these is discussed in turn.

Table 2.1

A Comparison of Oklahoma's Women Inmates to Women and Men Imprisoned in State Facilities

| | Oklahoma | State Jurisdictions | |
	Women	Women	Men
Total number in prison	975	36,211	617,181
Median age	32	27	28
African American/Black	37%	46%	45%
Hispanic	2%	12%	13%
American Indian	9%	.9%	.8%
Asian	---	.4%	40%
White	48%	40%	40%
Other races	4%	.7%	.9%
Married	27%	20%	20%
Mothers/fathers	95%	76%	60%
Median age 1st child born	18	18	
Median number of children	2	2	2
Physically abused	74%	53%	
Physically abused as juveniles	37%	37%	
Physically abused as adults	69%	23%	
Sexually assaulted	55%	36%	
Sexually assaulted as juveniles	39%	22%	
Sexually assaulted as adults	38%		
Use of alcohol	70%	74%	
Ever use drugs?	66%	72%	80%
Use of cocaine/crack	44%	42%	49%

Table 2.1 (continued)

	Oklahoma	State Jurisdictions	
	Women	Women	Men
Use of marijuana	76%	46%	56%
Use of speed	30%	25%	31%
Participation in drug treatment	26%	33%	29%
High school diploma/GED	64%	28%	38%
Vocational/technical school	66%	50%	
Some college	39%	15%	11%
College degree	10%	2%	
Median age at first arrest	22	17	17
Average number of times arrested	6	3	
Average number of times imprisoned	1.9	3	
Percent arrested as juveniles	34%	43%	
First imprisonments	54%	32%	19%
VIOLENT OFFENSES:			
Murder	15%	13%	11%
Manslaughter	3%	7%	3%
Kidnapping	1%	1%	2%
Rape	---	.2%	4%
Other sexual assault	---	.9%	5%
Robbery	8%	11%	21%
Assault	2%	7%	8%
Other violent offenses	---	1%	1%
Total current violent offenders	29%	41%	55%
Number on death row	5	45	2,550

Table 2.1 (continued)

| | Oklahoma | State Jurisdictions | |
	Women	Women	Men
PROPERTY OFFENSES:			
Burglary	4%	6%	17%
Larceny/theft	23%	15%	6%
Motor vehicle theft	3%	1%	1%
Arson	---	1%	1%
Fraud	2%	17%	3%
Stolen property	6%	2%	2%
Other property offenses	---	---	1%
Total property offenders	38%	42%	31%
DRUG OFFENSES:			
Possession	8%	4%	3%
Trafficking	9%	7%	5%
Other drug offenses/unspecified	10%	1%	.2%
Total drug violators	27%	12%	8%
PUBLIC ORDER OFFENSES:			
Weapons	1%	1%	2%
Other public order offenses	---	4%	4%
Total public order offenses	1%	5%	6%
--- indicates zero or a minuscule figure			

Sources: Figures in this table were extracted or derived from: the Project for Recidivism Research and Female Inmate Training (1991) Site 1 data; American Correctional Association (1990); Bureau of Justice Statistics (1991b); Bureau of Justice Statistics (1991a&f); Bureau of Justice Statistics (1988b); Streib, Victor L. (1991, March 5); NAACP Legal Defense and Education Fund, Inc. (1992) and Facts on File (1992)

Age and Racial Demographics

Given that Site 1 is a mixed-security-level prison that includes all of the state's maximum security female prisoners as well as medium and minimum security prisoners, we would expect that its residents would be older on average than residents in strictly minimum- or medium-security-level prisons. The median age for our sample at Site 1 confirms this. The median age of our sample (32 years) is 5 years greater than the national median age for women inmates.

Our sample at Site 1 has a larger proportion of whites and Native Americans than is reported for women nationally. This is partially the result of the rather unique demographics of the state. Oklahoma has an African American population of only about 7 percent and a Native American population of around 10 percent. Hispanic and Asian Americans together account for only about an additional 3 percent of the state's population. Given these demographics, we see that all groups, with the exception of African Americans, are either underrepresented or equitably represented in the Site 1 sample. Of particular note is the relatively high proportion of white women inmates in the state compared to nationwide figures. This basic demographic fact may account for a number of differences found in our sample as compared to national figures. For example, the high levels of educational attainment and first-time imprisonment correlate with the high levels of white women imprisoned in Oklahoma. African American women prisoners, who are overrepresented in our sample, are discussed in more depth in Chapter 6.

Marriage and Motherhood

Over one-quarter of our sample at Site 1 report being married. This compares to only one-fifth of the national female inmate population. Additionally, an astounding 95 percent of the Site 1 sample are mothers, which is substantially greater than the reported three-quarters of national female inmates and three-fifths of national male inmates who are parents. Many of these differences can undoubtedly be explained by the fact that women in the Site 1 sample are older. Nevertheless, the picture that emerges from the sample is that these women are more likely to be both wives and mothers than is typically the case for women inmates nationwide. We emphasize, however, that the vast majority of the women in our sample, as well as the national female inmate population, are single mothers. An important question for future research is, What happens to the children?

Physical and Sexual Abuse

Nearly three-quarters (74%) of the women in our sample report being physically abused at some point in their lifetime. This rate is much higher than the approximately one out of two rate for imprisoned women nationally. When broken down by age of occurrence, there is not much difference noted in physical abuse before the age of 18 between our sample and the national female inmate population. Indeed, the proportion is the same (37%). The big difference comes in the occurrence of physical abuse during adulthood. In our sample, seven out of ten (69%) of the women report physical abuse as adults as compared to only about a quarter of the national sample (23%). Indeed, on close examination, the pattern is reversed for our sample and the national female inmate population with regard to age of occurrence. The national population shows physical abuse to be more prevalent before adulthood, while our sample shows it to be more prevalent during adulthood.

Sexual assault differences between our sample and the national female inmate population display much the same pattern as do physical abuse differences. Over one-half of our sample report being sexually assaulted either as an adult or as a juvenile: this compares to a little over one-third for the national female inmate population. Unfortunately, we were unable to gather national data on adult sexual assault, but it is instructive that the rate of juvenile sexual assault is nearly twice as high in our sample (39%) as in the national population of women inmates (22%). We suspect that this pattern also holds for female prisoners who were sexually assaulted as adults, although we are unable to confirm this. In Chapter 5, we discuss our findings on abuse more thoroughly.

Drug Use Pattern

Although there does not appear to be a significant difference between our sample and the national population of women prisoners on the use of alcohol (70% compared to 74%) or drugs (66% compared to 72%), there is an overall pattern that suggests that drug use is lower in our sample. For example, the reported proportion of our sample that have used cocaine, marijuana, and speed are all lower than the reported levels among the national population of female inmates (42% to 49% cocaine use, 46% to 56% marijuana use, and 25% to 31% use of speed, respectively). Additionally, just over a quarter of our sample report participating in a drug treatment program, as compared to a third of the national population of women inmates. In total, although drug use and abuse is extraordinarily high in both our sample and the national population of women prisoners, there is comparatively less drug use among our sample than among the general population of female inmates. Chapter 4 gives further information about drug usage in our sample and among women in general.

Educational Attainment

Probably the most striking difference between our sample and the national population of women inmates is the degree of educational attainment evidenced by the former. Almost two-thirds of our sample (64%) report having either a high school diploma or the GED. This compares to only 28 percent of women inmates nationally. These differences persist at all levels of education. Two-thirds of the sample at Site 1 report some vocational or technical school training, as compared to one-half of women inmates in the national population. More dramatic, however, are the differences in the rate of college attendance and degree attainment. Two-fifths of the women in our sample report some college in their background, as compared to approximately one out of seven women in the national population (15%). Furthermore, fully one out of ten women in our sample report a college degree of some sort, as compared to only one out of fifty women in the national population. In short, the women in our sample are substantially better educated than the national female inmate population.

Age at First Arrest and Rate of First Imprisonment

Not only is the median age of the women in the Site 1 sample older than the national female inmate population, but the median age at first arrest is older. Indeed, the gap of five years exists both at current median age and age at first arrest between the two distributions. In essence, women in our sample are not only older while they are imprisoned, but they were also older when they were first arrested. While we are not certain, there may be a link here with the fact that over one out of two women in our sample report being imprisoned for the first time (54%) as compared to approximately (32%) serving their first imprisonment.

Violent and Drug Offenses

Nationally, a startling 41 percent of all women in prison are imprisoned because of violent offenses. Among our sample of imprisoned women, 28 percent are there for violent offenses. In contrast, one out of eight women nationally was imprisoned for drug offenses, while in our sample over one out of four was imprisoned for drug violations (27%). This indicates that in our sample, drug offenses are a substantial contributor to women's imprisonment in the Site 1 facility—more than they are nationally. Indeed, in the Site 1 facility drug offenses are as much a contributor to incarceration as are violent offenses. This is in clear counterdistinction to the national pattern for women inmates, in which violent offenses are more than three times more likely than drug offenses to be the reason for incarceration. More attention to the centrality of patterns of drug use and incarceration is paid in Chapter 4. Insights about violence against women in Chapter 5 and Chapter 7 may explain violent offenses among women prisoners.

QUESTIONS FOR RESEARCH

The following are some of the questions that guided our research efforts and the corresponding chapters in which these questions are examined.

- What are the primary characteristics of women prisoners? (Chapter 2)

- In what ways do levels of self-esteem affect female recidivism? (Chapter 3)

- Do women who experience a sense of control over their lives recidivate less? (Chapter 3)

- In what ways does education affect female recidivism rates? (Chapter 3)

- What effect does the presence of support systems have on recidivism? (Chapter 3)

- How are drug use and female recidivism related? (Chapter 4)

- How does a history of abuse affect the likelihood of recidivating? (Chapter 5)

- Are there significant ethnic differences among women inmates that need to be considered when developing programs to combat recidivism? (Chapter 6)

- Is the death penalty a warranted option for female violent offenders? (Chapter 7)

- What perspectives about organization are useful for enhancing the effectiveness of prison institutions? (Chapter 8)

- What influence do the attitudes of correctional staff have on female recidivism? (Chapter 9)

- Does successful adaptation to prison lessen the chances of recidivating? (Chapter 10)

- How do public and private patriarchy affect a women's likelihood of becoming criminal or recidivating? (Chapter 11)

The remaining chapters explore these intriguing questions. Our preliminary research findings present important insights about women in prison and raise additional questions that need future examination.

3   Self-Esteem and the Woman Prisoner

Constance Hardesty, Paula G. Hardwick, and Ruby J. Thompson

In developing an accurate profile of female inmates and assessing future life chances, it is essential to explore the issue of self-esteem. While the term self-esteem is used interchangeably with self-respect, self-love, self-worth, positive self-concept, and positive self-image, there is no consensus for a definition of self-esteem in the literature. Sanford and Donovan (1984) provide concise definitions that are useful for the purposes of this chapter. They define *self-concept* or *self-image* as "the set of beliefs and images that we all have and hold to be true of ourselves" (p. 7). One's level of *self-esteem* is, therefore, the measure of how much one likes and approves of one's self-concept (Sanford & Donovan, 1984).

Benson and Mullins (1990) and Pugliesi (1989) relate increased self-esteem to the experience of success in one's life. Because women tend to internalize blame for lack of success rather than recognize the social structural constraints to their success in our society, self-esteem can be severely affected (Benokraitis & Feagin, 1986). This chapter explores the relationship between self-esteem and the experiences and characteristics of women prisoners.

Research has consistently reported that an inmate's self-esteem just prior to release is an indicator of the inmate's potential to recidivate (Bennett, 1974; Dukes & Lorch, 1989; Fletcher, Moon, & Rolison, 1992; Gendreau, Grant, & Leipciger, 1979; Goldsmith, 1987; Hairston, 1991; Rosenberg & Rosenberg, 1978). By providing a moderating effect on the rate of recidivism, self-esteem can positively affect the inmates' children, other family members, temporary caregivers, and the public, as well as the inmate. Thus, it is important to understand the factors within the individual's background and current life context that influence her level of self-esteem. Understanding the factors that contribute to self-esteem may enable the development of programs, policies, and institutional environments that promote individual growth in self-esteem and hence improve life chances and the quality of life.

While research has explored the issue of self-esteem and prison populations, it has primarily focused on male inmates. Many of the factors influencing self-esteem may be consistent for both males and females; however, gender differences in social expectations and lived experiences may create substantial differences as well. This chapter draws on previous male-based offender research and in addition is grounded in an understanding of women's life contexts and research on the self-esteem of women in the general population. The chapter adopts an exploratory approach, using bivariate analysis to examine the relationship between individual factors and self-esteem among women prisoners. Several factors are examined in our exploration: the inmate's individual and family characteristics and social support during incarceration, childhood background, problem behaviors and life context prior to incarceration, and family and individual experiences while incarcerated. The results of our analyses of these factors are presented at the end of the chapter.

INDIVIDUAL AND FAMILY CHARACTERISTICS AND SOCIAL SUPPORT

Respondents' characteristics that may affect self-esteem include internal/external locus of control, family structure, social support, education, and socioeconomic status. *Internal/external locus of control* refers to the extent to which a person perceives life events as being contingent upon one's own actions (internal) or upon chance, fate, luck, or powerful others (external). Research indicates that individuals with an external locus of control tend to have lower levels of self-esteem, while those with an internal locus of control tend to display higher levels of self-esteem (Fitch, 1970; Harrison, Guy, & Lupfer, 1981; Love, 1991; Ryckman & Sherman, 1973). The analysis in this chapter explores the relationship between self-esteem and locus of control among female inmates.

Family structure defined in terms of marital status and number of children may also be important in relation to self-esteem among female inmates. Research indicates that societal expectations play an important role in influencing one's self-concept (Singh, 1970). A woman's self-esteem is related to how well she conforms to her internalized societal gender-role concepts (Benson & Mullins, 1990; Broverman et al., 1972). These social roles provide opportunities to create and maintain supportive relationships and to experience success, or efficacious action, in life (McCall & Simmons, 1978; Pugliesi, 1989; Rosenberg & Rosenberg, 1978). Harrison, Guy, and Lupfer (1981) found that the family is a primary source of satisfaction among women. It is logical to expect that family would be important to incarcerated women as well. For example, Widom (1979) states that self-esteem and acceptance of social roles do not differ between incarcerated and nonincarcerated women. Further, LeFlore and Holston (1989) found that offender mothers are as acculturated into the parenting roles as nonoffender mothers and have the same perceptions of their socially ascribed roles as noncriminal mothers of similar ages, education, socioeconomic status, and marital status, although they concede that disparity may exist between attitudes and actual behaviors. This research indicates that family is important in the lives of women due to social expectations as well as other factors. Based on this previous research, the present analysis explores the relationship between self-esteem and family structure in terms of marital status and number of children.

Social support is also related to self-esteem. Dukes and Lorch (1989) found that lack of family closeness, poor communication, value conflicts, and the unavailability of support contribute to low self-esteem. Low self-esteem, in turn, is related to "deviant" behavior, including substance use, in an attempt to compensate for lack of family closeness, poor communication, value conflicts, and the unavailability of support (Dukes & Lorch, 1989; Hawton, 1986; Hendin, 1985; Thompson, 1989). Our analysis examines the relationship between self-esteem and perceived social support in terms of the inmate's self-report of the number of friends she has and the number of the people who support her.

In regard to *education,* Dukes and Lorch (1989) found that low academic achievement can have a negative effect on one's self-concept, which in turn precipitates psychological problems and behavioral deviance. In contrast, Hannum, Borgan, and Anderson (1978) actually found that female offenders with higher levels of education possess lower levels of self-esteem. This study incorporates a measure of education to examine the relationship between level of education and self-esteem.

Research indicates that it is also important to examine the process by which *socioeconomic status* influences self-esteem and behavior. Studies have found that the direct relationship between low self-esteem and deviant behavior is especially strong among those within the lower socioeconomic levels (Gendreau, Grant, and Leipciger, 1979; Goldsmith, 1987; Rosenberg & Rosenberg, 1978). This analysis includes a self-reported measure of socioeconomic status.

In addition to the individual and family-related variables just specified, this study includes several additional variables to gain a more comprehensive understanding of the factors related to self-esteem among female offenders. The additional variables incorporated into this analysis are age, race, and perceived health status.

CHILDHOOD BACKGROUND

Widom (1991) indicates that there is a strong relationship between childhood delinquency and adult criminal behavior. She found that of the factors of delinquency, childhood victimization, and foster care placement, the most significant contributing factor to adult criminal behavior is childhood delinquency. Widom's study is important for the present analysis not only because of its specification of particular relationships between criminal behavior and other factors but also because it stresses the importance of examining childhood background factors in offender research.

While Widom's research focuses on childhood experiences and adult criminal behavior, information that connects adult criminal behavior, childhood background, and self-esteem is scant. This chapter addresses this inadequacy by examining the relationship between several childhood factors and the level of self-esteem of women prisoners. The major variables explored in Widom's study are included in our analysis. In regard to child caregivers our analysis measures whether or not the respondent was cared for primarily by parents. Childhood delinquency measures are included: age at first arrest, age at first incarceration, and whether or not the respondent was in a juvenile facility. Childhood victimization is included in terms of the physical, emotional, and sexual abuse experienced by the respondent as a child. Several additional childhood factors are included as well. These factors are geographic mobility during childhood, family size as a child, perceived social class experienced as a child, and whether or not the respondent was a teen mother.

INDIVIDUAL FACTORS PRIOR TO INCARCERATION

While an understanding of individual and family characteristics and childhood background are important in the study of female offenders and self-esteem, it is also essential to explore the inmate's life context as an adult prior to incarceration. One area examined by this study is employment history. Pugliesi (1989) found that employed women have higher rates of self-esteem and lower rates of depression and stress than unemployed women. Similarly, other research has found that the net effects of employment on the well-being of women are positive. Employment generally enhances feelings of well-being by allowing women to provide income to the household (a social imperative for the head of the household) and by increasing their network of social interaction and support (Pugliesi, 1989). To ascertain the relationship between self-esteem, employment, and related economic issues for female offenders, our analysis includes measures of whether or not at the time of her arrest the respondent was employed, receiving welfare assistance, and the sole provider for self and/or family.

Another aspect of the respondent's life context that must be considered is that of substance abuse. Thompson (1989) shows that substance abuse has negative long-term effects on peer relationships and self-esteem. This analysis examines the relationship between self-esteem and the respondent's perception that she has drug or alcohol problems. It is assumed that problems with drugs and/or alcohol were a part of the individual's life context prior to incarceration. This study also takes into account the adult life context by measuring the level of physical, emotional, and sexual abuse experienced by the respondent during her adult years.

FAMILY-RELATED ISSUES AS EXPERIENCED WITHIN THE INSTITUTION

Although institutional statistical data on marital and parental relationships are sparse, research indicates that incarceration severely stresses family ties. Hairston (1991) states that 75 percent of male inmates married at arrest were divorced at the time of her study. The impact of prison visitation on actual maintenance of the marital relationship was examined by Burstein (1977), who found that conjugal visits for male inmates were related to a significant decrease in marital difficulties.

Research demonstrates the positive role of the family in preventing recidivism. Holt and Miller (1972) show that only 2 percent of the men who had three different visitors during the year before parole were reincarcerated within one year of parole. This contrasts with 12 percent of men who had no contact with family or friends. Other studies have found positive correlations between visitors and postrelease success as well (Adams & Fisher, 1976; Glaser, 1969).

The continuity of family relationships experienced within the institution may be particularly significant in regard to parent-child relationships. Incarcerated parents express great concern over the potential loss of family relationships, particularly with children and spouses (Hairston, 1991). Fox (1982) states that mothers described their inability to visit with their children "as one of the most difficult and demoralizing experiences of confinement and viewed the loss of legal custody of one's children as a cause of depression, not only for the mother but for other mothers within the facility" (p. 7). Koban (1983) and McGowan and Blumenthal (1978) found that loss of their role as mother was one of the most traumatic factors in the adjustment of women offenders to institutionalization. Based on this research, our study takes into account family-related issues as experienced within the institution. We consider the frequency of family and children's visits in our study. We also explore the relationship between the inmate's participation in the parenting role and her self-esteem. Included are measures of whether or not the mother helped to decide who would keep her children, whether or not her parental rights were taken away, and whether or not she is satisfied with where her children are living.

INDIVIDUAL ISSUES AS EXPERIENCED WITHIN THE INSTITUTION

Gendreau and colleagues (1979) demonstrate the negative effects of incarceration on offender self-esteem over time. After measuring the self-esteem of male inmates following incarceration, they note a significant decrease when it is again measured prior to release. However, gender differences may exist in patterns of self-esteem of inmates. Tittle (1973) reports that women experience lowered self-esteem during incarceration with an increase prior to release, and Hannum and colleagues (1978) found an elevation in the self-esteem of female offenders over the course of imprisonment.

Worrall (1989) describes the paradoxes inherent in women's roles within the social structural and correctional systems, which contribute to lowered self-esteem. One example is the conflict between the need to financially provide for the family and the expectations to conform to a socially ascribed role of femininity and motherhood that does not prioritize employment. Correctional systems typically reinforce traditional roles, offering few vocational and educational opportunities for women within prison (Hairston, 1991; LeFlore & Holston, 1989; Worrall, 1989). A greater understanding of the relationship between institutional factors and self-esteem may facilitate the development of more appropriate programs and policies.

While this study is not longitudinal, it does explore the impact of institutional experiences. Specifically, we examine the relationships between self-esteem and whether or not the respondent has received education, counseling, and adequate health care while incarcerated.

MEASUREMENT

To examine mean self-esteem scores by specific individual, family, background, and institutional factors, the variables are coded into categorical variables. All of the demographic variables, including *age, education, marital status, socioeconomic status*, and *race*, are self-reported variables recoded into categories based on frequency distributions. *Number of children* is the combined total of biological and adopted children recoded into four categories. *Locus of control before incarceration* and *locus of control after incarceration* are measured by two separate questions in which the respondent could choose from five responses ranging from "events in my life are . . . completely out of my control" to "events in my life are . . . completely in my control." Similarly, respondents were asked to respond to the statement, "I am *healthy* according to five categories ranging from (1) completely false to (5) completely true. *Number of friends* and *number of supportive people* are straightforward, open-ended variables recoded into four categories (0, 1–3, 4–10, >10).

Background factors, including who was the *primary caretaker, geographic mobility*, and perceived *socioeconomic status* during childhood, are all self-reported categorical variables recoded into four or fewer categories. *Age at first arrest, age at first incarceration*, and *number of siblings* are all straightforward, open-ended items recoded into four categories. *Juvenile facility* is a dummy variable with "yes" indicating a positive response to the questions, "Did you spend any time in a juvenile facility?" *Teen mother* is a dummy variable recoded from an open-ended measure of age at first child's birth with "yes" indicating that the respondent's first child was born before the respondent was 18.

Respondents were asked how often they were *physically abused before the age of 18, emotionally or mentally abused before age 18, physically abused after the age of 18,* and *emotionally or mentally abused after age 18*. Respondents selected from four response categories ranging from never to frequently. Respondents also were asked *how often they were sexually abused or raped before age 18* and *how often they were sexually abused or raped after age 18*. Responses included 12 categories ranging from never to "more than ten times." Based on frequency distributions, these variables were recoded into four categories: (1) never, (2) once, (3) 2–10 times, and (4) over 10 times. The abuse variables for before age 18 are included in the analysis of childhood background factors, while the abuse questions for over age 18 are included in the analysis of adult-life-context variables.

Additional adult-life-context variables are developed from yes/no questions. These include the following:

- *Sole provider*—At the time of your arrest, were you the sole provider for your household or yourself?
- *Welfare*—Were you receiving welfare assistance at the time of your arrest?
- *Drug problems*—Do you think that you have a problem with drugs?
- *Alcohol problems*—Do you think that you have a problem with alcohol?

Employment is a yes/no variable developed from open-ended work history questions.

Regarding family experiences within the institution, respondents were asked several questions in regard to each child. If respondents answered "no" for any child to the question "Did you decide or help decide who would keep this child when you were incarcerated?" then the variable *decision on child placement* is coded "no." If the respondent answered "yes" for any child to the question "Have your parental rights been taken away since you have been incarcerated?" then the variable *parental rights removed* is coded "yes." If the respondent answered "no" for any child to the question, "Are you satisfied with where your children are?" then the dummy variable *child residence satisfaction* is coded "no." Respondents were asked for each child "How often do your children visit?" The five response categories provided ranged from "never" to "weekly." The variable *frequency of children's visits* is a measure of the highest frequency reported for any of the children. Frequency of *visits from other family members* was asked using the same categories and has been recoded into three categories labeled (1) never, (2) occasionally, and (3) often.

In regard to other institutional experiences, respondents were asked, "Have you received treatment for (a) alcohol problems, (b) drug problems, or (c) emotional problems while incarcerated?" The "yes" response to the *emotional treatment* variable indicates that the respondent did receive treatment. The *drug treatment* and *alcohol treatment* variables are recoded into three categories as follows: (1) The respondent perceives that she has a problem but did not receive treatment, (2) the respondent perceives that she has a problem and did receive treatment, and (3) the respondent perceives that she does not have a problem. All respondents indicating that they have a drug problem received treatment, so there are no cases in the second category. Respondents were asked to answer "yes" or "no" to whether or not they had experienced *health problems* while incarcerated. They were asked if they had received treatment for all, most, some, few, or none of their health problems. The *health treatment* variable is recoded into two categories as follows: (1) some, most or all and (2) few or none. *Education while incarcerated* is a yes/no variable developed from a series of questions asking if and when (relative to incarceration) the respondent attended and/or graduated from high school or college.

Self-esteem is a five-item Likert scale based on items asking the respondent how true or untrue she feels it is that she (a) is a good person, (b) is a nice person, (c) is a friendly person, (d) likes herself, and (e) is easy to like. Each item has a five-point range from (1) "completely false" to (5) "completely true." The Cronbach's alpha for the index is .829.

RESULTS

Table 3.1 provides the mean self-esteem scores by specific individual and family factors. The basic demographic variables, age, education, marital status, and number of children, do not indicate significant differences in mean levels of self-esteem. The social class measure indicates a higher level of self-esteem for middle and upper-middle classes than for lower class, though the difference is not statistically significant. Similarly, though the difference is not statistically significant, African American women report higher levels of self-esteem than other women inmates.

Table 3.1 reports that an individual's sense of general health is related to self-esteem. Those who answer "completely true" to the statement, "I am healthy" report significantly higher levels of self-esteem. Similarly, and consistent with previous research, individuals who report the highest level of internal control report greater self-esteem. This difference is statistically significant. It is interesting that only the inmate's sense of internal control before incarceration is related to self-esteem. The sense of being in control of life events while incarcerated is not related to self-esteem.

Also significantly related to self-esteem is social support. Those reporting the greatest number of friends and supportive individuals have higher levels of self-esteem. It is also interesting and paradoxical that those relying on no one for support or friendship report significantly higher levels of self-esteem.

Table 3.2 presents mean self-esteem scores for several childhood background characteristics. Most of the background characteristics, including family size, perceived social class during childhood, the experience of being a teen mother, age at first incarceration, age at first arrest, and

Table 3.1
Mean Self-Esteem Scores by Individual and Family Factors

Variables	Mean Self-Esteem
Age	
18-25 years	21.8
26-30	22.4
31-35	22.1
>35	21.6
Education	
< H.S.	22.4
H.S. or GED	22.0
Some college	21.6
College degree or higher	21.6
Marital Status	
Married	20.0
Not married	22.0
Number of Children	
0	21.4
1	22.5
2-3	21.8
4 or more	22.3
Perceived Economic Group as Adult	
Poor to lower middle class	21.4
Middle class	22.3
Upper-middle to upper class	22.2
Race	
Black	23.0
Native American	21.3
White	21.3
Other	21.4
Perceived Health* ("I am healthy.")	
Completely false	18.0
Mostly false	19.8
Partly false	21.1
Mostly true	21.3
Completely true	23.4
Social Support	
Number of Friends*	
0	22.7
1-3	21.5
4-10	21.5
>10	22.9
Number of People who Support Me*	
0	24.0
1-3	21.4
4-10	21.4
>10	22.9

Table 3.1 (continued)

Variables	Mean Self-Esteem
Locus of Control	
"Before I came to prison, I thought events in my life were _____ my control.*	
Completely out of	21.9
Mostly out of	21.9
Partially in	21.8
Mostly in	21.7
Completely in	23.4
"Since I came to prison, I believe that events in my life are _____ my control."*	
Completely out of	21.8
Mostly out of	22.3
Partially in	21.5
Mostly in	22.1
Completely in	22.5

*Differences between group means significant at $p < .05$.

spending time in a juvenile facility, are not significantly related to self-esteem. It is interesting that while the difference is not significant, children who were cared for primarily by their fathers report higher levels of self-esteem. In line with previous related research, those raised by foster parents or institutions report the lowest levels of self-esteem.

There is a statistically significant relationship between childhood geographic mobility and self-esteem. Individuals who experienced geographic stability, moving zero times before age 18, have the highest level of self-esteem. Those inmates who experienced ten or more moves during this time period have the lowest levels of self-esteem. This finding fits well with those reported in Table 3.1 regarding support and locus of control. That is, geographic stability may enhance the development of relationships and support networks important in the lives of women and may provide a sense of stability and control over life events.

Measures of both physical and emotional abuse are directly related to self-esteem. Clearly, higher levels of abuse experienced by female inmates in adolescence, whether physical or emotional, relate to lower levels of self-esteem in adulthood. The frequency of sexual abuse follows the same pattern as the frequency of physical and mental abuse. However, the reported differences are not significant.

Table 3.3 explores the relationship between self-esteem and various characteristics of the inmate's life context prior to incarceration. In contrast to previous research, employment status is not related to self-esteem. Consistent with previous research, this finding suggests that the positive effects of employment on self-esteem do not carry over after the employ-

Table 3.2

Mean Self-Esteem Scores by Childhood Factors

	Mean
Caretakers (provided most care during childhood)	
Mother, mother and others, or stepmother	21.9
Father	22.4
Other relatives	21.9
Foster parents or institutions	20.8
Geographic Mobility*	
(By age 18, how many times had you moved?)	
0	22.7
1-3	22.1
4-9	22.0
10 or more	21.5
Family Size	
(With how many sisters and brothers were you raised?)	
0	21.3
1	21.3
2-3	21.9
4 or more	22.3
Perceived Social Class as a Child	
Poor to lower-middle class	21.7
Middle class	22.0
Upper-middle class	22.3
Teen Mother (Age 17 or less)	
Yes	22.3
No	21.8
Physically Abused before Age 18*	
Never	22.5
Once	22.8
Occasionally	21.0
Frequently	20.8
Emotionally and Mentally Abused < 18*	
Never	22.6
Once	23.0
Occasionally	21.6
Frequently	20.8
Sexually Abused or Raped < 18	
Never	22.3
Once	21.8
Occasionally	21.5
Frequently	21.1
Age at First Arrest	
< 18 years	22.0
18-22	21.7
23-28	22.5
29 or higher	21.7

Table 3.2 (continued)

	Mean
Age at First Incarceration	
< 20 years	21.8
20-25	21.9
26-30	22.3
31 or higher	21.8
Juvenile Facility	
Yes	22.2
No	21.9
*Differences between group means significant at p < .05.	

Table 3.3

Mean Self-Esteem Scores by Individual Factors Prior to Incarceration

	Mean
Employed Prior to Arrest	
Yes	22.0
No	22.0
Sole Provider at Arrest Time	
Yes	21.8
No	22.2
Welfare Assistance at Arrest Time	
Yes	22.2
No	21.9
Perceived Problem with Alcohol*	
Yes	20.9
No	22.3
Perceived Problem with Drugs*	
Yes	21.5
No	22.3
Physically Abused as Adult	
Never	22.7
Once	22.5
Occasionally	21.7
Frequently	21.4
Emotionally or Mentally Abused as Adult*	
Never	22.8
Once	22.4
Occasionally	21.7
Frequently	21.3
Sexually Abused or Raped as Adult	
Never	22.2
Once	21.9
2-10 times	21.7
Over 10 times	21.6
*Differences between group means significant at p < .05.	

ment ceases with incarceration. Additionally, women's financial situations as sole providers for their families and/or themselves or as recipients of welfare assistance at the time of incarceration are not related to self-esteem after incarceration.

Consistent with previous research indicating the negative aspects of substance abuse, the results of this analysis indicate that respondents who report that they have a problem with alcohol or with drugs report lower levels of self-esteem. The finding is statistically significant for both the alcohol problem variable and the drug problem variable.

As in the case of the variables measuring abuse experienced prior to age 18, the experience of physical and/or mental/emotional abuse in adulthood is significantly related to self-esteem. Higher levels of abuse are associated with lower levels of self-esteem. The frequency of sexual abuse or rape follows the same pattern but is not statistically significant.

Table 3.4 focuses on family-related factors as experienced within the institution. Previous literature stresses the importance of the maternal role and the associated social expectations in their impact on self-esteem. Given this previous research, a negative relationship between self-esteem

Table 3.4

Mean Self-Esteem Scores by Family-Related Factors as Experienced within the Institution

Variable	Mean
Helped decide who would keep all children	
Yes	22.0
No	21.9
Parental rights regarding any child taken away	
Yes	21.6
No	22.1
Dissatisfied with residence of one or more children	
Yes	21.9
No	22.0
Most often respondent sees one or more children	
Never	21.7
Seldom	21.5
Every few months	22.5
Monthly	22.3
Weekly	22.4
Visits from family members	
Never	21.5
Occasionally	22.1
Often	22.4
*Group means significantly different at $p < .05$.	

and loss of maternal roles and self-esteem would be hypothesized. However, the results in Table 3.4 do not support this argument. Those who helped to make decisions about the placement of their children, who have retained their parental rights, who are satisfied with the placement of their children, and who see their children more often do report higher levels of self-esteem. However, the differences in means are not statistically significant for any of these variables.

Table 3.5 examines mean self-esteem scores for other institutional experiences. Consistent with the previously discussed finding regarding health and self-esteem, those who indicate that they have experienced health problems while incarcerated report significantly lower levels of self-esteem. However, the perception that most or all of these health problems have been treated while incarcerated is not related to self-esteem. Similarly, those who report alcohol problems and who have received treatment do not report significantly different levels of self-esteem than those who have not received treatment while incarcerated.

Inmates who have received treatment for emotional problems report lower levels of self-esteem than those who have not received treatment.

Table 3.5

Mean Self-Esteem Scores by Individual Factors as Experienced within the Institution

Variable	Mean
Received Education	
Yes	21.5
No	22.4
Treatment for Alcohol Problems	
Have no problem	22.3
Have problem and received treatment	20.8
Have problem and received no treatment	21.0
Treatment for Drug Problems	
Have no problem	21.5
Have problem and received treatment	22.3
Treatment for Emotional Problems*	
Yes	21.1
No	22.2
Experienced Health Problems*	
Yes	21.4
No	22.6
Received Treatment for Health Problems	
Some, most, or all	22.0
Few or none	22.2

*Group means significantly different at $p < .05$.

Because there is no measure of whether or not the respondent actually has emotional problems, it is not possible to examine the differences between those with emotional problems who did receive treatment and those with emotional problems who did not receive treatment. Thus, the negative relationship is probably due to the fact that those receiving treatment are also those most likely to perceive themselves as emotionally unhealthy.

Those who report that they have received education at any level during incarceration actually report significantly lower levels of self-esteem. This is consistent with the previous finding reported in Table 3.1 regarding the negative relationship between education and self-esteem. In general, the results in Table 3.5 suggest that institutional programs as they currently exist are not related to high levels of self-esteem among female inmates.

DISCUSSION AND CONCLUSIONS

This chapter provides a basic understanding of the relationship between self-esteem and various individual, family, and childhood background characteristics. Several patterns have emerged regarding these relationships. These patterns focus on the respondents' sense of self as (1) an individual, (2) part of a family, (3) part of a social network, and (4) as a victim.

In regard to the sense of self as an individual, several factors are related to self-esteem. Individuals who perceive themselves to be healthy report higher levels of self-esteem. This finding indicates that in developing strategies to improve self-image, it is important to address the general health needs of individual women.

Additionally, the sense of self as an individual is important in regard to locus of control. Not surprisingly, those who believe that events in their lives were completely in their control before incarceration have higher levels of self-esteem. This finding indicates that institutional programs, as well as the general treatment of inmates, should be geared toward empowering women rather than controlling them. To increase a sense of internal locus of control, it is necessary to promote programs that encourage autonomy and self-responsibility.

Related to most individuals' sense of self is level of education. It must be noted that education is not significantly related to self-esteem in this study and that those who are more highly educated report lower levels of self-esteem. This finding, while counterintuitive, is actually consistent with the idea of congruency. Those with higher education may be experiencing a higher level of incongruence between their status as an inmate and the status they are expected to have achieved given their education.

Further, developing institutional programs to meet educational needs is not positively related to self-esteem, as noted in this study. These results suggest the need to reevaluate our educational programs within the institution and possibly to develop avenues for inmates to productively use their education as a means of promoting higher levels of self-esteem.

A second important theme addressed in this analysis is that of sense of family. As discussed, previous research has emphasized the significance of family roles and relationships in relation to women's self-esteem. However, within this study, none of the variables related to family relationships, control over family factors, or family structure are significantly related to self-esteem. This finding does not imply that family is not important to female inmates. On the contrary, family may be very important and significantly related to satisfaction or quality of life. However, the results do question the preoccupation with women's sense of self as primarily or exclusively tied to their roles of wife or mother. The findings clearly state that female inmates are individuals, not simply wives or mothers, and their sense of self is related to their sense of individual self first and foremost.

Thirdly, self-esteem must be considered in relation to the inmate's sense of social support. Individuals with higher numbers of friends and supportive people report higher levels of self-esteem. This finding is not surprising and is consistent with the idea that support networks provide a safety net and a means for individual development. Further, the negative relationship between childhood geographic stability and self-esteem may be related to social support. Individuals with more stability may have developed stronger networks and support systems. It is interesting, however, that individuals reporting zero friends and zero supportive people also have higher levels of self-esteem. It is possible that some inmates who report high levels of self-esteem may have mentally separated themselves from other people to develop a sense of higher individual status. In general, the findings encourage the promotion of friendships and support networks for female inmates.

A final pattern emerging in the data is the relationship between self-esteem and victimization. The greater the frequency of physical or emotional abuse experienced by the respondent, whether before or after the age of 18, the lower the level of self-esteem. This finding clearly supports the development of quality counseling programs dealing specifically with issues of physical and mental abuse victimization. Relating this finding to that of locus of control, it is important that programs dealing with abused inmates focus on the development of a sense of internal locus of control.

Also regarding victimization, those who are victims of their own substance abuse, whether drugs or alcohol, report lower levels of self-esteem. Again, this finding encourages the development of counseling programs and, more specifically, programs dealing with the promotion of a sense of internal locus of control.

One of the most significant findings in the analysis is that of institutional programs. For the most part, individuals who have received treatment while incarcerated have lower levels of esteem. This is not surprising in the case of treatment for emotional problems because those needing and receiving help may be those with lower self-esteem initially. It is surprising, however, that those who receive treatment for alcohol abuse within the institution have lower self-esteem levels than those who have an alcohol problem but do not receive treatment.

In sum, these findings warrant a reevaluation of institutional programs. The findings encourage the promotion of programs and policies that allow for the practical application of inmates' education and promote a sense of internal locus of control. It is essential that programs promote family relationships and support networks, but most important, they must focus on building the inmate's sense of self through her individual strength and not through society's stereotypical expectations of her as a wife, mother, or woman.

4   Patterns of Substance Use among Women in Prison

Dreama G. Moon, Ruby J. Thompson, and Regina Bennett

Research on drug abuse among female offenders is noticeably lacking. This gap stems from the tradition of using male subjects in human experiments and from the unexamined assumption that gender is not an important research variable (Ray & Braude, 1987). Although recent public attention has focused on the well-documented relationship between drug use and crime, the majority of the literature discusses this relationship only with respect to males. Until recently, most studies have excluded samples of women (Bureau of Justice Statistics, 1991c). In this chapter we will discuss: (1) substance use and abuse among women in general, (2) gender differences in substance abuse, and (3) substance abuse among women in prison.

Drug use and abuse are complex and difficult phenomena to study. The use of drugs changes over the life cycle of the individual and is affected by variables such as age, race, and class; the nature of these impacts are examined in this chapter. One of the most often used, and least precise, measures is lifetime prevalence, or "the use of one or more drugs over the course of a person's life" (Clayton et al. 1987, p. 83).

The number of women in prison in general is growing, and these numbers have been accompanied by an increase in the number of incarcerated female drug users. Between 1985 and 1988, the number of women in prison rose by 41 percent. It has been noted that women arrestees are more likely to test positive for drugs in general and more likely to test positive for cocaine or heroin in particular than are their male counterparts. If these trends are indicative of future patterns, it is crucial that we understand the unique factors that account for female drug abuse and criminality.

SUBSTANCE ABUSE AMONG WOMEN AND MEN

Definition of Terms

Reed (1985) defines *drug abuse* or *dependency* as the "compulsive or destructive use of many types of psychoactive substances, including heroin, prescription drugs, over-the-counter drugs, and alcohol" (p. 7). For the purposes of this chapter, we will use the terms *drug abuse, drug dependency*, and *substance abuse* interchangeably to refer to all forms of drug abuse (including alcohol abuse unless otherwise noted) except over-the-counter drug abuse. We use the term *gender* rather than *sex* to discuss the differences among adult male and female patterns of drug abuse in order to capture the social and cultural meanings as well as the biological ones associated with the terms "male" and "female" in our society.

The Relationship between Drugs and Crime

Drug use and crime appear to be connected. Three ways in which drugs are related to crime can be identified: (1) psychopharmacological, (2) economic-compulsive, and (3) systemic. *Psychopharmacological* refers to instances when a drug user commits a crime due to drug-induced changes in physiological functions, cognitive ability, and mood. *Economic-compulsive* refers to occasions when a drug user commits crime in order to obtain money with which to purchase drugs. *Systemic* refers to situations in which violent crime occurs as a part of the drug business or culture (Bureau of Justice Statistics, 1991c). While these factors are helpful in explaining many drug-related crimes, in the case of women, we need to consider other elements as well, such as general, or non-drug-related, economic necessity; coping strategies; and the level of drug use in the dominant culture in general. These elements set the stage for the use of drugs and potential involvement in crime. Although research indicates linkages between drug use and the commission of crime, it often neglects factors that offer explanation as to why people, particularly women, initially use drugs. Perhaps it is these elements on which we need to focus our attention if we are to understand the links between women, drugs, and crime.

One confounding factor may be the feminization of poverty and the increase in the numbers of female-headed households. Martin (1990) reports that in 1985, about one-half of all poor persons in the United States lived in families with female householders as compared to only about one-fourth of the poor in 1959. Martin goes on to explain that although poor women are as likely to be employed as nonpoor women, they are more likely to earn low wages, be underemployed, and receive less support from absent fathers than are nonpoor women. The impact of these economic realities is compounded by the presence of drug addiction. Sutker (1985) notes that the female addict is most likely a single parent with one or more dependent children. In light of these facts, it is reasonable to assume that female involvement in drug sales may frequently be economic in nature.

Miller (1990) offers another perspective. She suggests that "female substance abuse can be described as an attempt to control the perceived invasion of physical or psychological boundaries" (p. 186). She theorizes that a woman's physical and psychological spaces are often invaded without her permission, and in an attempt to dull the pain of these invasions, she self-medicates. This potential may be even stronger for a women who, by virtue of her membership in more than one oppressed group, is a likely target for higher levels of physical and psychological invasion. Miller (1990) says these invasions range from actual physical episodes, such as rape, battering, and incest, to "intrusions of family members who insist that the girl or woman give up her own needs to accommodate theirs [and] deny her right to mental privacy" (p. 186), to the patriarchal control of society that dominates all spheres of existence. Substance abuse and self-medication allow the user to distance herself from painful situations, control access to information about herself via "secrets," and control her anger. As Reed (1985) indicates, women more often report using drugs to cope with life, while men say they use drugs most often for pleasure or social reasons. Tucker (as cited in Sutker, 1985) also finds that addicted women are less likely than men to use social strategies to cope with unpleasant emotions and more likely to isolate and take drugs to cope with these feelings. In addition, research on female use of prescribed medication indicates that certain forms of substance use and/or abuse among women are supported and even encouraged by society. Clayton and colleagues (1987) report that men in a 1982 National Institute on Drug Abuse (NIDA) national survey had a higher lifetime prevalence than women for use of all types of drugs—except for prescribed drugs.

Another reason that women are increasingly involved with drug-related crimes is that society in general is more involved with drugs. Drug and alcohol addiction are among the most common and serious social problems in U.S. society. According to the NIDA 1990 National Household Survey on Drug Abuse, 37 percent (74.4 million) of Americans report some use of an illicit drug at least once in their lifetime. Furthermore, a major study funded by the National Institute of Mental Health finds that alcoholism is the most prevalent psychiatric diagnosis, while drug abuse or dependence is the third most frequently reported disorder (Hanson, 1991). Mirroring the dominant culture (i.e., male behavior), today's women are increasingly likely to use drugs and become active in drug-related crime.

Women involved in drug-related crimes often act in concert with their male partners. In other words, following her "man," the female offender exhibits behavior that she may not otherwise manifest. In their study of addicted males and females, the Women's Drug Research Project (as cited in Sutker, 1985) found that 85 percent of the African American women and 93 percent of the white women were living with men who were abusing drugs. As female identity is so often tied to the status of the men in their lives, women often cross many thresholds of acceptable behavior in the name of "love." Unfortunately, the male of the couple often determines the couple's social status, and consequently, if the male partner is involved in criminal activities such as drug abuse or sales, the woman is likely to be as well. Research indicates that women in prison are generally initiated into the "drug world" by their addicted male partners (Sutker, 1985). This may be the case especially for addicted women, given their tendency to value male roles, devalue female roles, and therefore seek to emulate male behavior (Reed & Noise, as cited in Sutker, 1985).

The aforementioned as well as other factors tend to work in combination, which further complicates the issue of female involvement in drug abuse and related crime. For instance, a single mother on welfare may elect to sell drugs as a way of increasing household income or of coping with life demands that she cannot satisfy. Later, she may become addicted to the drug, and then commit more crime as a means of feeding her habit. Whereas her initial impetus to engage in crime was based on family economic need or psychological distress, her subsequent decision to increase her criminal activities is related to meeting her addiction needs. Furthermore, the psychological impairment caused by her use of drugs makes her less likely to perceive and seek alternatives. Thus, her engagement in further criminal activity becomes based less on choice and more on need.

WOMEN IN PRISON AND DRUG ABUSE

Substance abuse may be the most serious corrections issue of the nineties. The correlation between women being incarcerated and substance abuse is staggering (Bureau of Justice Statistics, 1991f). Nationally, female involvement with drugs has dramatically increased in both personal consumption (abuse) and distribution and sales. This has resulted in an increase in female conviction and incarceration (Oklahoma Department of Corrections, 1989). Over the decade of the eighties, the number of women arrested for drug violations, including possession, manufacturing, and sales of illicit drugs, increased at about twice the rate for men: a 307 percent increase for women compared to a 147 percent increase for men (Bureau of Justice Statistics, 1991f). In both the 1979 and 1986 surveys of inmates in state prison facilities, the Bureau of Justice Statistics (1991f) found that the percentage of women in prison for drug-related offenses exceeded that of men (12 percent compared to 8.4 percent).

When compared to men, women in prison are more likely to have been using cocaine or heroin in the month before their offense occurred, more likely to have been using these drugs daily, and more likely to have been under the influence of major drugs at the time they committed the crime (Bureau of Justice Statistics, 1991f). Overall, almost half (46%) of the women in prison had been using drugs or alcohol or both at the time the imprisonment offense took place. Moreover, a third of these women reported prior participation in a drug treatment program (Bureau of Justice Statistics, 1991f).

Women in Prison, Drugs, and Recidivism

According to the National Institute of Corrections (1991), within the offender population, serious drug use fuels other criminal behavior. While there is some indication that involvement in crime precedes serious drug use, increased substance use appears to accelerate the level of criminal activity among those individuals already involved in crime. Drug addicts are involved in approximately three to five times the number of crime incidents as arrestees who do not use drugs, and they have a significantly greater number of arrests than non-drug-involved arrestees (National Institute of Corrections, 1991). In addition, once released from incarceration, drug-abusing offenders demonstrate a marked tendency to resume their criminal careers and to participate in what has come to be known as "the revolving door of justice." Punishment alone (i.e., without accompanying treatment) has not proven effective in changing the behavior of drug-abusing offenders, and it appears to have little impact on long-term drug use (National Institute of Corrections, 1991).

Drug Use Patterns of Imprisoned Women in Oklahoma

In a report by the Oklahoma Department of Corrections (1989), statistics compiled from a random sample survey of incarcerated women indicate the following:

1. Almost three-fourths (74%) of the women in Oklahoma prisons have used drugs sometime in their lives.

2. The most frequent types of drugs used are marijuana (44%), cocaine (28%), amphetamines (24%), heroin (15%), alcohol (13%), barbiturates (13%), PCP (9%), and LSD (8%).

3. Over half (52%) of the women were under the influence of drugs at the time of their immediate offense.

4. Four out of ten (43%) have received some type of counseling or hospitalization for drug abuse.

5. A little over a third (34%) have received treatment more than once.

6. The average age women began using drugs was 18 years.

THE PRESENT STUDY

Analysis of Data

We use tabular analysis to interpret our raw data. In particular, a number of categorical questions were asked on the survey administered at Site 1 regarding drug use history, perceptions of drug and alcohol problems, drug and alcohol treatment history, and perceptions of programs needed both while in prison and after release from prison.

Respondents were asked whether they had ever used nonprescribed ("street") drugs or alcohol, and "yes/no" response choices were provided. Respondents were also asked if they felt they had a problem with drugs or alcohol and chose between the answers "yes," "no," and "don't know." Questions were asked about participation in drug and alcohol treatment or counseling programs both before and during incarceration ("yes/no" response choices were provided). Write-in response questions were then asked about the kinds of programs respondents felt they needed both while in prison and after their release, as well as about what they thought caused their problems with the law.

We examined age, education, race, and history of physical and sexual abuse for association with drug abuse. *Age* is an open-ended measure coded into three categories: 18–24 years, 25–34 years, and over 35 years. *Race* was coded first using categories of "Caucasian" and "Other," and then using "African American/Black" and "Other." *Education* responses were recoded into "high school graduate" and "non–high school graduate." The high school graduate measure includes those with a GED. *Physical abuse* is measured by two items asking respondents to indicate, on a four-point continuum from "never" to "frequently," how often they had been physically or sexually abused before and after the age of 18.

Findings

Results reflect a high rate of drug use. This is consistent with results reported in the literature. Twenty-seven percent of our sample were incarcerated for drug-related offenses. This number is substantially higher than the national figure of 12 percent reported by the Bureau of Justice Statistics (1991f). Of the one-third who responded to the question, about half felt that drugs and/or alcohol were responsible for their legal problems. Seven out of ten respondents used alcohol prior to incarceration and almost that many (66%) used nonprescription ("street") drugs. Table 4.1 shows the level of drug use reported by our sample.

Variables

Education. Our data bear out previous research that links drug use and education. Sixty-four percent of our sample are high school graduates or holders of the GED. Non–high school graduates in our sample are more likely than high school graduates to have used nonprescription drugs (72% compared to 54%).

Race. Our analysis also reveals distinctive patterns of drug use among racial groups. The data indicate a positive relationship between white women and the use of a variety of drugs (alcohol, opiates, amphetamines ["speed"], tranquilizers, hallucinogens, and barbiturates ["downers"]), *excluding* cocaine and crack. The relationship between white women and the use of amphetamines, or "speed," and alcohol is particularly strong. This positive relationship holds true especially for white women between 25 and 34 years of age.

A positive relationship is found between African American women and the use of cocaine or crack, particularly for Black women over the age of 35 years. African American women in our sample are not as likely to use a wide variety of drugs as are white women. For example, very few African American women use amphetamines (4%) or barbiturates (9%) compared

Table 4.1	
Drug Use among Imprisoned Women at Site 1	
Alcohol	70%
Cocaine/crack	42%
Marijuana	46%
Amphetamines/"speed"	25%

to 40 percent (amphetamines) and 28 percent (barbiturates) for white women.

Self-Reported Drug Problems

About four out of ten women surveyed (39.6%) think that they have a problem with drugs, and about one-fifth (19.3%) report having a problem with alcohol. About one out of ten are unsure if they have a problem with drugs or alcohol (4% and 4.5% respectively). About a quarter (25.8%) of our sample report having received counseling or treatment for a drug problem prior to incarceration, and 13 percent received counseling or treatment for an alcohol problem before coming to prison. While in prison, 17.6 percent say they have received counseling or treatment for an alcohol problem, while 28.9 percent have received counseling or treatment for a drug problem. A positive relationship exists for those who think they have a drug or alcohol problem and their likelihood of having received treatment either prior to or after coming to prison. In addition, over a fourth of the respondents (27%) list some sort of drug and/or alcohol counseling or treatment as a programmatic need both while in prison and after release. It should be noted that many of the women included in their responses self-help groups like Alcoholics Anonymous and Narcotics Anonymous.

Self-Reported Abuse

In accordance with other research (cited by Sutker, 1985), our data indicate a positive relationship between history of childhood abuse and the likelihood of drug use. Regardless of race, the more frequently a woman was physically or sexually abused before the age of 18, the more likely she is to have used drugs and alcohol; however, white women reported more abuse than did African American women (Jackson, Carter, & Rolison, 1992). Surprisingly, physical abuse as an adult seems to have no relationship to propensity toward drug use except for the use of speed.

FUTURE RESEARCH DIRECTIONS

Our results indicate new directions for future research into the relationship between drug use and women in prison. The difference in drug use patterns by race is of particular interest. It is interesting to note that white women as a group tend to manifest a "smorgasbord" approach to drug use. This may be because access to a variety of drugs is more available to women of the dominant culture. On the other hand, African American women in our sample tend to be monodrug users. It is also noteworthy that there seems to be a preference for particular types of drugs along racial lines. As previously noted, white women tend to prefer amphetamines, or speed, whereas African American women used more cocaine or crack. This finding merits further investigation and has great ramifications for treatment planning.

For example, it may be that the old stereotype of the African American male heroin addict has been joined by that of the African American female crack user. We need to know if this pattern of drug use among African American women is geographically based or national. If the pattern does hold true nationally, we need to identify the factors in the African American woman's experience that puts her at such high risk. If the pattern is geographically limited, what is the difference in the experiences of Black women in different areas of the country? It may be that this drug-use pattern is not a local one and that there is a corresponding pattern of cocaine and crack use among incarcerated African American men, possibly because the Black community is targeted for higher crack sales. Another possible cause may be the stress and economic problems associated with single-female-headed households. Because there is a higher incidence of single-female-headed families in the African American community, it may be that more Black women are seeking the type of relief available through drug use. Martin (1990) reports that about one-half of African American families are female-headed households with one or more children under the age of 18. In addition, among those Black women who share a household with a man, 83 percent of the women live with men who abuse drugs (Sutker, 1985). It is not our intent in this chapter to offer an in-depth analysis of the variety of factors that impact African American women, but this drug use pattern merits close attention, especially given the ever-increasing numbers of incarcerated African American women; a new at-risk population may be developing.

CONCLUSIONS

The relationship between drug use and crime that has been reported in previous research is borne out in our study. The number of women incarcerated for drug-related crimes is increasing, and this growth is likely to continue unless intervention into the factors underlying women's involvement in drugs occurs. As the National Institute of Corrections (1991) indicates, drug offenders will usually return to criminal patterns of behavior after release unless their drug addiction is addressed while they are in prison.

It seems clear that a variety of factors exists that affects women's likelihood of using drugs, and these factors need to be considered when planning drug-treatment alternatives. Treatment options provided to women in prison may differ from those available for male prisoners. As distinctive education, age, and racial patterns of drug use among women are noted, programs will differ for women of various ages, educational levels, and ethnic backgrounds.

It is further suggested that treatment options for women with extensive childhood physical and sexual abuse histories require special consideration. Furthermore, due to the high incidence of relapse related to drug recovery in general, the success of these programs must be measured in ways other than recidivist statistics alone. Long-term follow up and multiple program accountability measures may provide us with a more realistic picture of the programs' success and shortcomings (National Institute of Corrections, 1991). Lastly, aftercare programs sensitive to the special needs of women who are drug-dependent offenders and staffed with drug and alcohol treatment professionals (including recovering former offenders) must be in place if they are to be successful. It must be emphasized that simply addressing a woman's drug problems alone will not ensure her success after release. Many factors other than drug dependency are related to her recidivism. By addressing social, economic, family, psychological, and addiction problems in combination, her potential for success after release is substantially enhanced.

5 Abuse and the Woman Prisoner

Elizabeth Sargent, Susan Marcus-Mendoza, and Chong Ho Yu

> Threatened he would kill me and my folks, screaming in my face, held gun to my head while having sex.
>
> —woman prisoner

In this chapter we will examine the history of abuse among female inmates. As reported in Chapter 2, 74 percent of the inmates at Site 1 reported being physically abused, and 55 percent reported being sexually assaulted. These statistics are significantly higher than those for the general population and for inmates in other prisons nationwide, and suggest that most of the inmates have been victims of one or more types of abuse. In order to develop programs for the women that adequately address their needs, it is necessary to examine the incidence and kinds of abuse and their correlates.

TYPES OF ABUSE

Before discussing abuse among women prisoners, it is important to define the types of abuse commonly perpetrated against women in the United States. Although physical, emotional, and sexual abuse are discussed separately, they often occur simultaneously, and the definitions overlap. For example, it is hard to imagine sexual or physical abuse that is not also emotionally abusive.

Incest

Children are frequently the victims of emotional, physical, and sexual abuse. Incest victims are also likely to have experienced emotional, physical, and sexual abuse. Butler (1978) defined *incest* as any act with sexual overtones perpetrated by a needed and/or trusted adult, whom a child is unable to refuse because of age, lack of knowledge, or the context of the relationship. They report multiple symptoms of incest, such as phobias, sleep disturbances, excessive bathing, obsessions, phobias regarding sexual matters, and public masturbation in children and adolescents. In older children, sexual abuse of younger children, seductive behavior toward adults, chronic urinary tract infections, venereal disease, pregnancy, delay or disruption of menstruation, vaginal, anal, or urethral bleeding are common. Adult female survivors of incest may exhibit compulsive behavior; severe difficulties with intimacy and trust; sexual problems; feelings of being "freaks"; poor body image; amnesia about parts of their childhood; guilt and shame; severe contempt for, hostility towards, and distrust of men, especially of one's own ethnic group; phobias about being touched (especially during gynecological exams); and fear of losing control (Butler, 1978).

Butler (1978) states that victims feel betrayed by the perpetrators and by other adults who fail to stop the abuse. Their development is interrupted, they experience loss of self-esteem, and they are unable to cope effectively with the multitude of feelings they are experiencing. As a result of their inability to unburden themselves of their awful secrets, they may engage in what is considered antisocial behavior. And as Garry L. Rolison discusses in Chapter 11, some of that behavior, such as running away, may serve to label them as "bad" or "criminal."

Battered Women

According to the Oklahoma Coalition on Domestic Violence and Sexual Assault (cited in Culpepper, 1991) battering or abuse can take four forms: physical, sexual, psychological, and destruction of property and pets. Physical battering includes all aggressive behavior by the offender to the victim's body. Sexual battering includes attacks on the victim's breasts or genitals or forced sexual activity, usually accompanied by either threat or actual physical battery. Destruction of property and pets is not random, but intentional and aimed at destroying objects of value to the victim. Psychological battering includes threats, controlling behavior, attacks on self-esteem, and intentionally frightening the victim. Psychological battering usually takes place in a relationship where there has already been at least one instance of physical abuse (Culpepper, 1991). For example, one of the inmates surveyed in our study reported that her husband beat her, ran her over, threatened to kill her children, and stole all her money. This reflects psychological and physical abuse as well as threats to deprive her of her children and money.

A study of battered women inmates who killed their abusers found that psychological battering included being isolated from friends and family, jealous accusations, and threats of death or harm to the women's family or children. Half of the women studied by Foster, Veale, and Fogel (1989) reported enforced isolation. Despite the physical injuries described by these women, half stated that mental abuse was far worse than the physical abuse. One woman states, "I would prefer to have my teeth knocked out than mental abuse" (Foster, Veale, & Fogel, 1989, p. 277).

The psychological effects of all forms of battering are debilitating and often mimic schizophrenia and borderline personality disorder. Rosewater (1985) states:

Misdiagnosis is a common problem for clinicians when they meet a battered woman, as unfortunately many clinicians are simply not educated about this problem. A major contribution of feminist therapy to the mental health field is the ability to view a woman and her problems in the context of the society in which she lives. However, this awareness of the impact of cultural conditioning on the emotional problems developed by women has yet to affect the diagnostic procedure used by mental health professionals. Nowhere is this lack of integration more evident than in the dearth of knowledge about the similarities between schizophrenic, borderline, and battered women and how to diagnose them differently. (pp. 215–16)

According to Rosewater, some of the characteristics battered women share with individuals who have schizophrenia are social isolation or withdrawal; marked impairment in role functioning as wage earner, student, or homemaker; blunted, flat, or inappropriate affect; digressive, vague, overelaborate, circumstantial, or metaphoric speech; and ideas of reference (paranoid ideation). Some of the forewarning and lingering signs of schizophrenia are also characteristic of battered women, but again, with far different implications in terms of diagnosis. While blunted, flat, or inappropriate affect can be a symptom of schizophrenia, it can also be a means of effecting calm or avoiding potential conflict. It is important to realize that battered women tend to develop skills to postpone anticipated violence (Walker, 1984). Odd or indirect communication may be adopted as a coping mechanism if the woman has learned that direct communication may result in the onset of battering (Rosewater, 1985).

Some of the characteristics battered women share with individuals with borderline personality disorder are impulsivity or unpredictability; unstable and intense interpersonal relationships; inappropriate, intense anger; uncertainty about issues related to identity; affective instability; intolerance of being alone; physically self-damaging acts; and chronic feelings of emptiness or boredom (Rosewater, 1985).

Further, Rosewater (1985) theorizes that given the violent reality of battered women's lives, these are understandable behaviors. The major difference is that the responses of battered women are often indicative of a clear grasp of their reality as opposed to the lack of connection with reality characteristic of individuals with schizophrenia. For instance, battered women are often seen as paranoid and delusional because they report events about which no one else is aware, or simply because they are extremely fearful with no apparent basis for fear. The fact that the source of the fear is not obvious to others (as in cases where the abuser is a respected member of the community) does not mean that it is not real. In addition, many battered women appear irresponsible, when in fact they often miss work or social obligations because they are embarrassed to be seen after they have been beaten.

INCIDENCE OF ABUSE

Because the nature of abuse inhibits the collection of accurate statistics (i.e., victims often do not report it, people are uncomfortable discussing it), it is impossible to accurately identify the amount of abuse that occurs. In fact, Culpepper (1991) in her discussion of domestic abuse demonstrates two different ways that the incidence of abuse is presented: estimated abuse and reported abuse. For instance, a total of 15,010 acts of domestic abuse were reported in Oklahoma in 1990. However, other sources estimate that a woman is battered every 15 seconds in the United States, and that 3 to 4 million American women are abused during pregnancy.

Battering is not the only underreported type of abuse. De Young (1987) reports:

The same confusion of reports and statistics exist in relation to other kinds of abuse as well. There has been a considerable amount of debate as to the extent of child molestation in society. Since there is no uniform method for the collection of data, and since there is every indication from research studies and from anecdotal evidence that child molestation is an underreported behavior, no reliable figures as to its true incidence in the general population can be determined. (p. 4)

For example, while Justice Department statistics for 1988 show reported child abuse and neglect rates of only 3.4 percent (Bureau of Justice Statistics, 1990b), other studies (mostly retrospective self report) estimate that from 12 percent to 38 percent of all women are victims of child sexual abuse (Russell, 1983), which is only one type of abuse.

CURRENT STUDY

Pollack-Byrne (1990) offers the following description of women inmates:

By all accounts, the lives of many prisoners before prison . . . involved economic distress, victimization, and self abuse through use of drugs and alcohol. Often, they have had a series of negative relationships with men, being either exploited or physically abused. Children come early, and the women typically have little in the way of skills or resources to take care of their children. The women's families often have similar instabilities and economic problems and are not able to care for the women's children either, although typically that is where children are placed. (p. 78)

As previously stated, very little research has looked at the connection between incarceration and abuse. Specifically, do female inmates report having experienced abuse of some sort more frequently than other women? It is striking to notice the similarities between the types of difficulties experienced by most women who have been abused and incarcerated. Given the overlap in descriptions, it would be expected that a significant number of abused women with high-risk profiles are, have been, or will be incarcerated.

Pollack-Byrne (1990) cites several studies that found a high incidence of a history of abuse among female inmates. These studies indicate rates of reported sexual abuse from 35 percent to 63 percent and physical abuse rates from 35 percent to 53 percent. Our study of inmates at Site 1 supports the contentions of Pollack-Byrne. This study explored frequencies of reported physical, sexual, and emotional abuse and the relation between abuse and education, drug and alcohol usage and abuse, and race, factors we thought might be important in developing programs for women in prison.

Two hundred and sixty-seven inmates were administered the survey in small groups; they answered the following questions about abuse:

83. Before age 18, were you physically abused?

84. Before age 18, were you emotionally or mentally abused?

85. Before age 18, were you raped, sexually abused, or molested?

86. Have you ever been physically abused by a mate, husband, boyfriend, lover, friend, acquaintance, or partner?

87. Were you ever emotionally or mentally abused by a mate, husband, boy-friend, lover, friend, acquaintance, or partner?

88. After age 18, were you ever raped (forced to commit sexual acts against your will)?

For our analysis, we coded the responses to each question into two categories: having never been abused, and having experienced abuse one or more times. Table 5.1 gives the frequency of each type of abuse reported by the inmates.

Since the survey questions of interest yielded categorical data, we used the chi-square test for all our analyses, and phi coefficients were calculated to ascertain the strength of the relation (percentages are presented in Table 5.2). First we examined the incidence of abuse and education. Inmates were asked whether they had (1) a high school diploma, (2) a GED, or (3) no high school diploma. Significant chi-squares were found when analyses were conducted on questions 83 (8.091, $p = 0.018$, phi $= 0.177$), 84 (9.702, $p = 0.008$, phi $= 0.194$), 85 (11.309, $p = 0.004$, phi $= 0.209$), and 86 (6.403, $p = 0.041$, phi $= 0.163$), but not on questions 87 and 88.

| Table 5.1 | | | |
| Percentage of Abuse | | | |
		Ever	Never
Q83	Before the age of 18, were you ever PHYSICALLY ABUSED?	37.45%	62.55%
Q84	Before the age of 18, were you ever EMOTIONALLY OR MENTALLY ABUSED?	43.88%	56.12%
Q85	Before the age of 18, were you ever RAPED, SEXUALLY ABUSED, or MOLESTED?	39.71%	60.83%
Q86	Before the age of 18, were you ever been PHYSICALLY ABUSED?	69.14%	30.86%
Q87	Before the age of 18, were you ever EMOTIONALLY or MENTALLY ABUSED?	69.58%	30.42%
Q88	Before the age of 18, were you ever been RAPED?	39.42%	60.58%

Table 5.2		
Education, Substance Abuse, Race, and Percentage Reporting Abuse		
	Reported Being Abused	Reported Not Being Abused
Had Obtained High School Diploma		
Q83	23.36%	38.41%
Q84	24.60%	39.39%
Q85	21.24%	40.69%
Q86	36.53%	26.67%
Perceived Problem with Drugs		
Q85	49.46%	36.43%
Q86	48.39%	27.14%
Q87	47.40%	30.40%
Perceived Problem with Alcohol		
Q85	26.88%	15.83%
Q86	24.18%	12.68%
Q88	29.03%	14.39%
Percentage Reporting Abuse by Race		
Q83		
African American	30%	
Caucasian	48.31%	
Native American	52.17%	
Q84		
African American	38.89%	
Caucasian	55.08%	
Native American	56.52%	

For questions 83, 84, and 85, which ask about abuse before the age of 18, we found that inmates who had never been abused were more likely to have a high school diploma than those who had been abused.

Overall, the percentage of inmates who did not have a diploma or GED ranged from 32 percent to 39 percent, indicating that many had earned a GED (many may have earned them in prison since most prisons require inmates to earn a GED if they have not graduated from high school).

For question 86, physical abuse after the age of 18, the relation was reversed. More of the women who reported being abused (36.53%) had high school diplomas than those who reported never having been abused (26.67%). Overall, the women who reported abuse were more likely to have a high school diploma or a GED. Only 29.94 percent of the former group had neither a high school diploma nor a GED, while 46.67 percent of the latter group had neither a diploma nor a GED.

Next, we looked at the relation between reported abuse and perception of having an alcohol or drug problem. In all cases, women who reported abuse were more likely to perceive themselves as having problems with drugs or alcohol. Significant chi-squares were found for question 92 ("Do you think that you have a problem with drugs?") and question 85 (3.907, $p = 0.048$, phi = 0.159).

Significant chi-squares were found for question 93 ("Do you think that you have a problem with alcohol?") and questions 85 (4.215, $p = 0.040$, phi = 0.135), 86 (3.985, $p = 0.047$, phi = 0.133), and 88 (7.396, $p = 0.007$, phi = 0.179).

In addition, we conducted analyses to find the relation between race and abuse. The three groups that were sufficiently represented among the inmates to be included in the analyses were African American, Caucasian, and Native American. Significant Chi-squares were found for race and questions 83 (8.229, $p = 0.016$, phi = 0.189) and 84 (5.951, $p = 0.051$, phi = 0.161).

Finally, we conducted analyses to determine whether there were interactions between the variables found to be related to abuse. We obtained significant Chi-squares for race and education (11.814, $p = 0.19$, phi = 0.227) and race and alcohol abuse (8.023, $p = 0.018$, phi = 0.196). The data indicated that while there was an approximately equal percentage of inmates from each race who have graduated from high school (African American 32.58%, Caucasian 33.05%, and Native American 34.78%), fewer African Americans (21.35%) obtained a GED than Caucasian (38.98%) or Native American inmates (43.48%). Therefore, more African American inmates (46.07%) did not have a high school diploma or its equivalent compared to Caucasian (27.97%) and Native American (21.74%) inmates. In examining the relation between race and alcohol problems, we found that fewer African American inmates (11.11%) perceived themselves as having an alcohol problem than Caucasian (27.62%) or Native American (27.27%) inmates.

DISCUSSION

A significant portion of the women surveyed at Site 1 report having been abused. In fact, 69 percent of the women reported physical and/or emotional abuse after the age of 18. The relation between abuse and education, drugs and alcohol, and race raise some interesting questions.

There was a significant relation between reporting abuse and earning a high school diploma or GED. Those inmates who reported being abused before the age of 18 were less likely to have earned a high school diploma than those who had not been abused. Inmates who had been abused were more likely to have earned a GED than a high school diploma either before or during incarceration. The percentage of inmates who had neither a diploma nor a GED was about even for those reporting abuse and those reporting no abuse. For those reporting physical abuse after the age of 18, the relationship is reversed. Inmates who had earned a high school diploma or GED were more likely to report having been abused.

There seems to be a pattern in which those reporting abuse before the age of 18 were not as likely to have earned a high school diploma as those not reporting abuse. As mentioned earlier, children who are being abused often have difficulty in school. Those inmates with a high school diploma were more likely to report physical abuse after the age of 18. This finding raises some interesting questions. We see a possible progression of reported abuse before the age of 18, reduced likelihood of obtaining a high school diploma or GED, and lowered frequency of reported abuse after the age of 18. Does this mean that by the age of 18, abuse had become a pattern in the lives of these women and thus was less likely to be recognized or commented on? That women abused as children are less likely to recognize abuse as abuse when it occurs in their adult lives? While these questions cannot be further clarified by this study, they would be important to address in future research.

Next, we examined the relation between reporting abuse and the perception of having a drug or alcohol problem. In every case, those who reported being abused were more likely to report having a problem with drugs or alcohol. Sexual abuse as a child or any type of abuse as an adult seemed to be related to the perception of having an alcohol or drug problem. This may mean either that those who have been abused and use drugs or alcohol use more of these substances or that they are more likely to perceive their usage as problematic. Drugs and alcohol may be a way that they cope or avoid coping with their abuse and/or the memories of it. This is consistent with the studies noted earlier in this chapter.

Finally, we examined the incidence of abuse by race. For physical and emotional abuse before the age of 18, we found reporting rates of 30–38 percent for the African American inmates, 52–57 percent for the Native American inmates, and 48–55 percent for Caucasian inmates. When we looked for an interaction between education and race and alcohol and drug problems and race, we found that 46 percent of African American inmates, as opposed to 28 percent of Caucasian inmates and 22 percent of Native American inmates had neither a high school diploma nor a GED. In addition, we found that only 11.11 percent of the African American inmates reported having an alcohol problem, compared to 27.62 percent of Caucasian inmates and 27.27 percent of Native American inmates.

Breaking down statistics according to race raises a whole new series of questions. For instance, African Americans overall reported less abuse and less trouble with alcohol and drug abuse. African Americans were less likely to have obtained a GED if they failed to graduate from high school. Since there are significant cultural differences between the three groups that we have not examined at this time, we do not wish to risk any unfounded assumptions, especially since we cannot distinguish between actual problems and perceptions or reports of problems. Again, this area is much in need of research.

Since a longterm goal of PRRFIT is to prevent recidivism, the research should be looked at with an eye toward development of programs that will enable the women to adjust to life "on the outside" with healthier coping skills. Therefore, we feel that programs in the area of alcohol and drug abuse, awareness of abusive patterns, and ways to break those patterns are essential. Indeed,

Our silence is the real crime, whether it's about battering, abuse in the penal system, legal abuse, sexism, racism, or any injustice. When women begin to take action, make decisions and set directions, they will change those conditions that violate us physically and emotionally and socially. Intervention is the key—when acted on it shows love and concern for one's self and other human beings, that will influence attitudes. Intervention states that violence and injustice against women is not accepted and won't be tolerated in any form. (Woman volunteer at the Women's Self Help Center, a former victim of battering; Bauschard & Kimbrough, 1986, p. 132)

One hopes programs will give women a chance to break their silence, heal their emotional wounds, improve their coping skills, and adjust to life outside prison. The research we have done for this chapter suggests that many women are most likely incarcerated as a result of abuse and its symptomology. We have demonstrated the need for further research and innovative programs that directly address the needs of incarcerated women.

6   African American Women in Prison

Deborah Binkley-Jackson, Vivian L. Carter, and Garry L. Rolison

Recent incidents such as the appointment of Clarence Thomas to the Supreme Court and the trial of Los Angeles police officers Powell, Wind, Koon, and Briseno are proof that sexism and racism are alive and well in America. Racism and sexism flourish in our nation's prison systems as well. A close look at women who are incarcerated indicates racial bias within the system (French, 1978). About one-half of all women incarcerated are African American, although only one out of eight women in the United States are African American. For two consecutive years (1989 and 1990), Oklahoma has incarcerated more African American women per capita than any other state with 500 or more women inmates (Bureau of Justice Statistics, 1989b). This chapter explains why this is the case and talks about the unique experience of the African American woman in Oklahoma prisons.

IMPRISONED WOMEN IN OKLAHOMA

Throughout Oklahoma's history, African American women have been incarcerated far more often than white women. In 1909 the Oklahoma State Penitentiary (the primary maximum security prison for men) in McAlester, Oklahoma, became the first prison in the state to house women inmates. Of the 17 women housed at McAlester in 1909, 8 were white and 9 were of African descent. In 1910, the total population of female offenders was reported to be 29 (10 white and 19 African American women).

The first women's prison in Oklahoma was built in 1926, also at McAlester, Oklahoma. The prison had a total population of 51. It was not until the early 1960s that the number of women inmates exceeded

68. This figure was not at all unusual for the state for most of its past history. The four women's facilities in Oklahoma house approximately 975 female offenders. While African American women comprise only 3 percent of Oklahoma's general population, they represent 41.4 percent of Oklahoma's female inmate population. White women comprise 52.5 percent of Oklahoma's female inmates and the remaining 6 percent are of other races, predominantly Native American, who represent 4.7 percent.

AFRICAN AMERICAN WOMEN IN PRISON

The percentage of imprisoned African American women is staggering not only in Oklahoma but throughout the nation as well. Much attention has been given to the large numbers of African American men who are incarcerated, but little attention has been paid to the number of African American women in prison. This is despite the fact that Bureau of Justice Statistics (1989b) indicate that African American men make up 48.7 percent of the total male prison population while African American women make up 49.2 percent of the total female prison population. In other words, despite the heavy focus on African American male imprisonment, more African American women are incarcerated, relatively speaking, than their male counterparts. In state prisons, the concentration of African American men and women is even greater than at the federal level; combined, African Americans of both sexes make up 50.4 percent of all inmates incarcerated in state facilities.

Table 6.1 indicates the female prisoner population under state and federal jurisdiction by race, according to state, and shows the incarceration rates of white and black women for institutions with a population of 500 or more. From the table we see that the state of Oklahoma leads the nation in the incarceration rate of African American women. Three out of every 1,000 African American women in the state of Oklahoma are in prison.

Oklahoma shares with Arizona the dubious distinction of having the highest incarceration rate of white women. African American women, however, are incarcerated at nearly nine times the rate of white women.

These numbers clearly indicate that the state of Oklahoma is a crucial location in which to conduct research on the difference among black and white incarcerated women.

Table 6.1

Incarceration of Women by Race According to State

	Prison Population			Incarcerations Per 1000	
	Total	White	Black	White	Black
U.S.	40,646	19,426	19,269		
Fed.	4,435	2,613	1,696		
State	36,211	16,813	17,573		
AL	845	326	519	.2	.2
AZ	780	580	164	.4	3.1
CA	6,000	3,401	2,175	.3	2.0
CT	647	214	286	.1	2.0
FL	2,551	1,026	1,520	.2	1.7
GA	1,110	414	693	.2	.2
IL	1,019	353	605	.1	.7
IN	624	406	216	.2	.9
LA	693	160	538	.1	.8
MD	728	189	537	.1	.9
MI	718	394	324	.2	1.1
MN	1,586	522	1,029	.1	1.5
NC	843	355	456	.1	.6
NJ	866	261	531	.1	1.0
NY	2,485	1,266	1,137	.2	.7
OH	1,995	778	1,217	.2	2.0
OK	975	512	404	.4	3.4
PA	944	390	550	.1	.1
SC	929	303	625	.3	1.0
TX	2,069	837	948	.1	.9
VA	794	264	523	.1	.8

NOTE: States presented in this table are those states with prison populations over 500 and excluding the District of Columbia.

SOURCE: Bureau of Justice Statistics, Correctional Populations in the United States, 1989.

CURRENT STUDY

Method and Sample

The first stage of the Project for Recidivism Research and Female Inmate Training, completed in spring, 1991, was a survey conducted at Site 1. This facility is a maximum security prison for women, although it is a residence for minimum and medium security offenders as well. The survey was developed after a review of previous Oklahoma Department of Corrections staff input and the feedback from several psychologists. An initial pilot survey was conducted on a small number of women of postincarceration status who were on parole and had a history of recidivism. A second pilot test, using 20 women inside the facility, was then conducted at the research site. A total of 15 revisions occurred before the final administration. The final instrument consisted of 142 closed and open-ended questions.

There were a total of ten survey sessions. The time of administration was between one-and-one-half and two hours. A total of 283 surveys were collected from the 330-inmate population. Of these, 14 surveys were eliminated due to inconsistencies (e.g., inmates completing two surveys, with data inconsistencies). The final data base was 269 completed and usable surveys. This represents a response rate of 82 percent.

Research Results

In our analyses we examine differences between African American women and white women inmates. We employ descriptive statistical techniques and logistic models. Although discriminant analysis may appear to be a more appropriate multivariate technique for distinguishing group membership, some of the variables that descriptively distinguish African American women and white women inmates do not evidence equal variance-covariance matrices. Because of this, discriminant analysis may produce suboptimal results.

Of the 269 respondents to our survey, 246 women (91%) gave self-reports of their racial background. The racial breakdown of our sample is as follows: 48.4 percent of the women reported that they are white or Caucasian; 36.6 percent, Black or African American; 9.3 percent, Native American or American Indian; 2 percent, Hispanic, Latino, or Mexican American; and 3.7 percent, "other." There were no Asian American women represented in this sample. State demographics indicate that African American women are overrepresented, white women underrepresented, and

Native American and Hispanic women equitably represented in the sample.

Salient Differences. There are five general areas in which African American women differ from white inmates in our sample:

1. Family and marital background
2. Age at first arrest and incarceration
3. Drug use before incarceration
4. History of emotional and physical abuse
5. Self-esteem

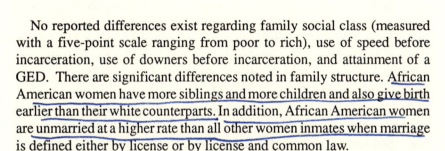

No reported differences exist regarding family social class (measured with a five-point scale ranging from poor to rich), use of speed before incarceration, use of downers before incarceration, and attainment of a GED. There are significant differences noted in family structure. African American women have more siblings and more children and also give birth earlier than their white counterparts. In addition, African American women are unmarried at a higher rate than all other women inmates when marriage is defined either by license or by license and common law.

African American women inmates were arrested and incarcerated at earlier ages than whites. Additionally, the two groups differ in their pattern of drug use before incarceration. White inmates report using speed and downers more than other female inmates, while African American inmates report using crack or cocaine more than other women inmates.

To assess emotional and physical abuse, we developed a four-item index in which we asked the respondent (1) whether she had been physically abused before the age of 18, (2) whether she had been physically abused after the age of 18, (3) whether she had been emotionally abused before the age of 18, and (4) whether she had been emotionally abused after the age of 18. Each item was measured on a four-point continuum ranging from "never" to "frequently." The Cronbach's alpha for the index is .762. African American women reported less abuse than did white women.

An index was also constructed to measure self-esteem. That index is comprised of six items asking the respondent how true or false it is that she (1) is a good person, (2) is a nice person, (3) is a friendly person, (4) is easy to like, (5) likes the way she looks, and (6) likes herself. Each item is measured using a five-point continuum from completely true to completely false. The Cronbach's alpha for the index is .815. African American women had a lower mean score on the index than did white women. The reversal of the index indicates that African American women inmates report a higher sense of self-esteem than do white inmates.

In summary, we find that African American women inmates have more siblings and more children and have given birth at a younger age than white women inmates. In addition, African American women inmates are unmarried at rates higher than all other inmates. Inmates of color were arrested and incarcerated for the first time at earlier ages than their white counterparts. Furthermore, the two groups differ in drug use before incarceration. White inmates are more likely than other inmates to have used speed and downers, while African American inmates are more likely than others to have used crack or cocaine. African American women inmates are less likely than white women inmates to report a history of physical or emotional abuse and more likely to report higher levels of self-esteem. Finally, African American female inmates and white female inmates do not differ with respect to having received a high school diploma (31% to 33%, .10/1 df). However, there is a significant difference noted in GED attainment (40% to 26%, 4.8/1 df).

Logistic Models. Based on the descriptive differences noted above, a logistic model was specified with the log odds of an inmate being white, the dependent variable in the first model, and the log odds of an inmate being African American, the dependent variable in the second model. For predictors we used both dummy and continuous variables. In particular, dummy variables were used to indicate whether an inmate was married, used crack or cocaine before incarceration, used speed before incarceration, used downers before incarceration, and had attained a GED. We used continuous variables to measure number of children, number of siblings, age at first arrest, and scores on our physical and emotional abuse and self-esteem indices. Thus, we specify as predictors those variables that we found descriptively differentiated between African American women and white women inmates. Age at first incarceration is not included in the model because of possible collinearity problems. We ran two models to see whether these differences exist for African American women and all other women inmates as well as between white women and all other women inmates.

The logistic results shown in Table 6.2 indicate that the model fits the data for whites (X^2 = 161.44/60, prob. = .453) and for African Americans (X^2 = 135.48/160, prob. = .921) quite well. In short, we find that type of drug used before incarceration, number of siblings, age at first arrest, and self-esteem differ between women of color and white women inmates.

Our major finding is in how well the model predicts racial membership between African American and other female inmates. Except for GED

Table 6.2

Logistic Regression Predicting Racial Membership of Oklahoma Female Inmates in a Maximum Security Facility

	White	Black
Intercept	1.854 (1.087)	-.641 (1.328)
Married	.148 (.217)	-.513* (.260)
Coke	-.638* (.232)	.722* (.237)
Speed	.595* (.239)	-1.224* (.409)
GED	.141 (.219)	-.347 (.254)
Downers	.773* (.290)	-.615 (.383)
Number of Siblings	.290* (.090)	-.203* (.084)
Number of Children	.248 (.130)	-.283* (.135)
Age at First Arrest	-.089* (.026)	.065* (.029)
Self-Esteem	-.135* (.068)	.157* (.078)
Abused	-.080 (.058)	.165* (.067)

NOTE: -2 log likelihood 161.44   df 160   N 170   135.48   df 160   N 171
*Indicates that the coefficient is significant at the .05 level.

attainment and the use of downers before incarceration, all of the model predictors are significant. In other words, the variables that we found earlier to be predictive of difference between white inmates and women of color are for the most part the variables that differentiate between African American female inmates and others.

DISCUSSION

This study has attempted to identify factors that differentiate African American women and white women inmates. Five dimensions of difference were found. Those dimensions are family structure, age at first arrest and incarceration, drug use before incarceration, exposure to physical and emotional abuse, and self-esteem. The factors that differentiate white inmates from others are also the factors that differentiate African American inmates from others. This is not unexpected, given that African Americans represent seven out of ten nonwhite inmates. However, the fact that the logistic model fits marginally better for Black racial membership may suggest that other incarcerated women of color are more similar to whites than to African American inmates in the five dimensions.

Implications

The findings of this research suggest that there are some differences noted between inmates that must be taken into account programmatically. For instance, given the differences in family structure noted for African American inmates, it is not unreasonable to expect that programs designed to involve inmate families pay particular attention to the African American family. We can expect this family to be less nuclear and possibly more extended in orientation than other families (Billingsley, 1968). Other factors to be considered are the increasing rates of marital termination and high rates of single-parent families within the African American community (Blackwell, 1991). Also, because of the possibility of the existence of the extended family, the potential within the African American family exists to involve many different family members to help support the inmate. Conversely, such findings draw our attention to the possible need to rely less on the family for nonblack inmates, in other words, to be more focused programmatically on developing support services outside the family for these women.

Within prison, programs are similarly affected. Differences in history of drug use, the incidence of emotional and physical abuse, as well as different levels of self-esteem all point to the need for different levels of intervention for African Americans and nonblack women inmates. Drug abuse education and treatment should emphasize cocaine for Black women and speed for white women. Likewise, programs designed to boost self-esteem and handle the aftermath of emotional and physical abuse might be better received (not necessarily more needed) by nonblack female inmates. Certainly the issues here may be quite different for the two groups, and at the very least programmatic intervention could be made more relevant by incorporating these differences.

We stress that although we have found group differences among women inmates in our sample, there are probably more similarities than differences. As researchers and practitioners, we are struck by how similar many of the experiences of inmates are regardless of race, age, or other broad demographic markers. We have intentionally drawn out differences in this chapter to help target program interventions. However, we remain ever mindful that all women prisoners suffer from neglect in our penal institutions and that programs of any type are minimal. Therefore, we do not want to overemphasize differences between African American women and white women inmates or lose sight of the fact that most programmatic interventions would be equally beneficial for both groups. Our attempt here is to sensitize practitioners to group differences that would aid in tailoring programs for maximum effectiveness and relevancy.

7   Women on Death Row

Kathleen A. O'Shea

> Not everyone on death row is guilty, not everyone is, but you don't go
> into trial as a person innocent until proven guilty, you go in guilty until
> you prove yourself innocent . . . and anyone who says it isn't true has
> never been there.
>
> —Woman on death row, May 1992

The United States has the largest group of condemned women on death
row in its history. As of March 1, 1992, there were a total of 45 women
known to be on death row in 17 states (NAACP, 1992), and of these
women, 5 (11.1%) are in Oklahoma. (The total includes four women in
Ohio whose clemencies were reversed in February 1992 [*Facts on File*,
1992].) No other "advanced" country in time of peace has had a greater
percentage. Yet we know very little about these women. The public hears
about women on death row, due to media fascination when they are
arrested and when they are executed, but otherwise, they remain invisible.
The high number of women on death row needs to be examined more
closely if we are to understand what is happening with women in our
criminal justice system today.

Victor L. Streib (1991), a professor of law at Cleveland State University
who has for a number of years been researching the imposition of death
sentences and the execution of females throughout American history,
indicates that the number of women offenders on death row nationwide
remained fairly low during the early 1980s until, for reasons yet to be
explored, in 1989 the number suddenly doubled (see Figure 7.1).

In the 36 states that mandate capital punishment, women may be
hanged, shot by a firing squad, given cyanide gas to inhale, electrocuted,

Figure 7.1

States With Women on Death Row

1982

1992

Sources: Adapted from information provided by the NAACP (1982; 1992)

or given poison through an intravenous drip (Bureau of Justice Statistics, 1990). If all the women who are on death row in the United States were executed today, 18 would be electrocuted, 3 would be gassed, and 24 would die by lethal injection.

In 1972 Chief Justice Thurgood Marshall postulated that given enough information about the death penalty, the "great mass of American citizens would conclude that the death penalty is immoral and therefore unconstitutional" (Sarat & Vidmar, 1976). It is not the purpose of this chapter to decide whether or not this might be true. The purposes are (1) to give historical background on the death penalty and how it has been applied to women in the United States, (2) to profile the women who are currently on death row and the conditions under which they are held, and (3) to propose some hypotheses from these findings for further research.

In the context of this chapter, the following definitions will prove useful.

An *appeal*, according to De Sola (1988), is a request by either the defense or the prosecution that a case be removed from a lower court to a higher court so that a completed trial can be reviewed by the higher court. *Capital crimes* are crimes punishable by death, and *capital punishment* is the death penalty (De Sola, 1988). A *contact visit* is a visit where the inmate is allowed to be in the same room with the visitor, and thus have physical contact (hugs, kisses, etc.). *Habeas corpus* is a Latin term that literally means "you may have the body." It has to do with a prisoner's right to be brought before a court so a judge may decide on the legality of his or her detention (De Sola, 1988). A *felony* is a crime punishable by imprisonment for more than a year or by death (De Sola, 1988).

U.S. HISTORY OF EXECUTING WOMEN

Though Margie Velma Barfield, a 52-year-old grandmother who died by lethal injection in North Carolina on November 2, 1984, is the only woman executed since executions resumed in 1977, the United States has a history of executing women. According to Schneider and Smykla (1991), women represent 2.5 percent of all persons executed under state and local authority since 1608. Ninety percent of these women were executed under local authority (counties, townships, villages), and the majority (87%) prior to 1866. These women were executed for a number of offenses, most notably witchcraft and poisoning of husbands.

The first woman known to have been executed in the United States was Jane Champion, in James City County, Virginia, in 1632. She was hanged for an unknown crime, and her age was not recorded (Schneider & Smykla, 1991). The youngest person on record executed in the United States was a female, Hannah Ocuish, age 12, a Native American hanged in New London County, Connecticut, on December 20, 1786, for the murder of a six-year-old white girl (Schneider & Smykla, 1991). Schneider and Smykla (1991) also mention Marja Lamb, a slave woman who was burned for arson in Suffolk County, Massachusetts, on September & 22, 1681, and Amy Spain, a 17-year-old slave who was hanged on March 10, 1865, in Darlington County, South Carolina, for an unknown crime. The oldest woman known to have been executed was a 65-year-old slave remembered only by the surname of Greene, who was hanged in Prince William County, Virginia, on February 13, 1857, for murder (Schneider & Smykla, 1991).

These early executions were public and usually held in town squares. Other than for the express purpose of being executed, women were not expected to attend. Women who did attend were considered indecent (Masur, 1989). This meant that women who were executed were not allowed the comfort of having female members of their families present in their final moments. Condemned women were forced to face execution before large crowds of men, who quite often came for the carnival atmosphere. Executions were carried out almost immediately, or at the very least within a few days, after sentencing. The concept of death row as we know it today did not exist.

By the 1830s, executions were no longer a public spectacle. State legislatures, influenced by abolitionists' outcries, moved them from town squares to behind prison walls (Mackey, 1976; Masur, 1989). In 1847, a group of Philadelphia women petitioned the legislature with over 10,000 signatures to abolish capital punishment (Masur, 1989). What they stated then seems by all accounts to hold true today: it is the poor who are executed, while the wealthy universally escape the death penalty.

CAPITAL PUNISHMENT

In the prologue to his 1986 ethnographic study of capital punishment, Otterbein states that capital punishment is the most extreme form of privileged force or physical coercion, the ultimate coercive sanction. He defines capital punishment as the "appropriate killing" of a person who has committed a crime against a community (p. 9). The three elements he deems necessary for an "appropriate killing" are that the killing must be within the community, it must be stated as appropriate by the laws of the community, and there must be a reason for the killing, that is, the person must have done something that violates the norms or mores of a culture.

In an opinion poll called "Attitudes of Oklahomans toward the Death Penalty" taken by the Department of Sociology at the University of

Oklahoma in December 1988, 63.2 percent of the Oklahomans polled were "strongly in favor" of the death penalty for persons convicted of first degree murder. On the issue of whether they favored life sentences without the possibility of parole over the death penalty, 49 percent said they did, while 47.9 percent said given the choice, they would prefer the death penalty (Center for the Study of Crime, Delinquency, and Social Control, 1988).

Because executions are held behind locked doors, in dark places, and before extremely small audiences, the vast majority of the people who favor the death penalty are never touched by it personally. The likelihood of any of us knowing someone on death row in our lifetimes is actually quite rare. Unlike fires, accidents, cancer, or heart attacks, the death penalty does not usually happen to a member of your family. Yet people are frequently sentenced to death in this country, and increasingly, some people receiving these sentences are women.

Researchers have long been aware of certain patterns in death sentencing practices in the United States. Quite often a death sentence depends not so much upon the crime as upon where it was committed and who committed it (Griswold, 1971; Gross & Mauro, 1983; Parisi, 1982; Paternoster, 1983; Zalman, 1976). African Americans are punished more severely than whites, the poor more severely than the rich, and women more severely than men (Radelet & Pierce, 1985; Kleck, 1981; Kruttschnitt, 1982; Zeisel, 1981; Wolfgang & Riedel, 1973; Judson et al., 1969).

During the 1970s and 1980s, about half of the people on death row in any given time were African American (Bedau, 1984; Bureau of Justice Statistics, 1989a). In Texas, African Americans who kill whites are six times more likely to receive the death sentence than African Americans whose victims are African American. In Florida, African American offenders who kill whites are 40 times more likely to end up on death row than whites who kill African Americans (Bedau, 1984; Lewis et al., 1979). In 1984 Bedau noted that of the 3,862 persons executed between 1930 and 1980 in the United States, 2,077, or 54 percent, were African American.

Categorically, women are more likely to be sentenced to death on a first offense than men (Bureau of Justice Statistics, 1990; Schmittroth, 1991). Although some studies have been done on how gender differences influence the sentencing and treatment of adult criminals (Steffensmeier, 1980), this needs to be looked at more closely as the number of women being given the death penalty increases. If a woman accused of a capital crime wants to avoid the death penalty today, she must be able to afford the best legal defense, investigators, and expert witnesses that money can buy. Chief Justice William O. Douglas commented in Furman v. Georgia that "one searches our chronicles in vain for the execution of any member of the affluent strata of this society" (Furman v. Georgia, 1972, p. 2733).

A person may receive the death penalty for any felony indexed by the FBI, including robbery, rape, burglary, grand theft, vehicle theft, and arson, if it is committed in conjunction with a homicide (Bailey, 1991; Bureau of Justice Statistics, 1990). In the state of Oklahoma, a person may be given the death penalty for:

- Murder with malice aforethought.
- Murder arising from specified felonies: forcible rape, robbery with a dangerous weapon, kidnapping, escape from lawful custody, first degree burglary, and arson.
- Murder when the victim is a child who has been injured, tortured, or maimed. (Bureau of Justice Statistics, 1990)

Since the 1990s, there have been an average of four cases per year in which an entirely innocent person is convicted of murder, and many of these people have been sentenced to death (Alexander, 1983; Bedau, 1982; Radelet & Bedau, 1988). As the number of executions increases each year, so will the probability of error. Therefore, it is safe to assume that innocent women are sitting on death row today. The injustice bears looking at, since the ultimate enactment of the penalty of death is irreversible.

Our Court Systems

The vast majority of people sentenced to death in the United States, historically as well as currently, have been convicted of some type of felony murder (Bailey, 1991). As a society, we choose to believe that the women who are on death row are there because they have committed the most horrible and unspeakable crimes (Auerbach, 1974; Suval & Brisson, 1974). However, the reality is that while this may be true in a few cases, the majority of these women have committed crimes that cannot be distinguished from the crimes of hundreds of others who are living out life terms in our state and federal prisons or who are now walking the streets, having received time off for good behavior. In many cases, two people equally involved in the same murder are given unequal sentences. We need to ask, Why is this?

Our system of death sentencing is one reason for this inequality. It can be compared to a game of chance whose winners are determined by the luck of the draw. The ethnic and economic background of the accused, the region in which the crime occurred, the attitudes of the police and the prosecutors, the skills of court-appointed lawyers and public defenders, and the personal prejudices of judges and juries are all variables in this deadly game (Davis, 1978; Frankel, 1973; Haney, 1984; Hogarth, 1971; Kaplan, 1985; Knowlton, 1953; Kroll, 1987; O'Donnell, Churgin, & Curtis, 1977; Whinery, 1976).

A number of states, including several southern states with the nation's highest execution rates, use a system of appointing lawyers from a list of local attorneys. Many are either young attorneys fresh out of law school or older ones who ordinarily specialize in title searches or divorce litigations. It is rare to find a court-appointed lawyer who is skilled in all the complexities of capital cases. Harold G. Clarke, Chief Justice of the Georgia Supreme Court, who has reviewed many death sentences, stated, "This is a highly specialized area of law, and even a good criminal lawyer may not have had much experience in capital cases" (cited in Lacayo, 1992). A study of the Texas judicial system found that three out of four convicted murderers with court-appointed lawyers were sentenced to death, as opposed to one out of three with private attorneys (Amnesty International, 1992). Aside from everything, court-appointed lawyers work for very little pay, and it is safe to assume that few, if any, know much about why women commit crimes. Lack of experience, little pay, and a poor understanding of women offenders do not add up to a good defense.

Under rules established by the United States Supreme Court in 1977, lawyers in criminal cases must recognize potential violations of fair procedure as soon as they occur and raise their objections at that time in the court. If they fail to do this during the trial, they may forfeit any chances their client has to raise those issues on appeals. Some of the most deadly mistakes or omissions are made during the "penalty phase" of a trial, when all the skills of an expert lawyer are called into play.

The penalty phase is a separate hearing following a guilty verdict, where the jury in capital cases chooses between a prison sentence and the death penalty. Prosecutors submit evidence of "aggravating factors," such as excessive cruelty, to convince the jury that the convicted killer should be executed. Defense lawyers are supposed to present "mitigating factors," such as evidence of abuse or a history of abuse, that might lead the jury to choose a life sentence. This is a crucial stage for many women. Of the 45 women on death row today, almost half (approximately 49%) have a history of abuse and are there for the murder of an abusive spouse or lover (O'Shea, 1992).

Although evidence of abuse is admissible in most courts, investigating abuse in a client's past is time-consuming and expensive. It often requires the services of social workers, psychologists, and special investigators, which poorly funded public defenders cannot afford. The case of Judith Haney, a woman on death row in Alabama for murdering her husband, is an example. Haney is appealing her death sentence because her former court-appointed trial lawyers failed to obtain hospital records of her treatment for injuries that were inflicted by her husband. Her attorney feels that if the jury could have appreciated the role of abuse in the life of Haney and her children, it would have been a very strong mitigating factor (Lacayo, 1992). To further harm her case, one of her court-appointed trial lawyers was held in contempt of court by the presiding judge and jailed for being intoxicated during her trial. Some death row inmates have been successful in appealing their cases on the grounds that they received ineffective counseling. However, with already overcrowded court dockets, most have not.

Left alone by the higher courts, no two juries and no two judges are alike. Applications of the law vary from county to county, from state to state, from court to court. Some judges and states hand out the death penalty more frequently than others. Judges have no clear rationale for sentencing, nor do federal or state laws provide adequate guidelines for them to follow (Williams, 1979). Federal Judge Marvin E. Frankel (1973), a prominent critic of sentencing practices, asserts that nothing in a judge's training or experience prepares him or her for understanding criminals and that judges are not uniformly humane and compassionate. He believes that relatively few judges have any experience in defending criminals and almost no judges have experienced the socioeconomic conditions under which offenders have usually lived. This lack of parallel experiences should cause us concern, as judges make irrevocable decisions about women's lives. To further complicate matters, these decisions are based on circumstances that are not always clear-cut: the extent of a woman's participation in a murder, whether she was provoked by anything such as abuse, her sanity, and whether or not she poses a future threat to society.

Although all five of the women on death row in Oklahoma are convicted of murder or conspiracy to murder, two of them were not present when the murders were committed, two may or may not have been present when the murders were committed, and only one was actually seen and identified at a murder scene (Clay, 1988; Mecoy, 1988; "Tahlequah Man," 1982).

In what Zimring and Hawkins (1986) refer to as "advocacy research," regional influences are emphasized as the most powerful factors in death sentencing and executions. Since the 1880s executions in southern states have exceeded the numbers in other regions (Schneider & Smykla, 1991). From 1935 to 1969 southern states executed 1,887 persons, the highest numbers being from Georgia, Texas, and Florida (Zimring & Hawkins, 1986).

Although no studies have appeared about how southern attitudes toward women may influence the likelihood of a woman being sentenced to death, it is worth noting that the states with the highest numbers of women on death row are southern. Both Florida and North Carolina currently have six women on death row, while Alabama and Oklahoma have five.

Abolition and Reinstatement of the Death Penalty

By 1853 Michigan, Rhode Island, and Wisconsin had abolished the death penalty. By 1929, sixteen states had abolished the death penalty (Zimring & Hawkins, 1986). In 1972 the Supreme Court, by a 5-4 vote, banned capital punishment as it was then practiced in the United States. In reaching a decision in the case of Furman v. Georgia, the Court stated that "the imposition and carrying out of the death penalty" constituted cruel and unusual punishment and was in violation of the Eighth and Fourteenth Amendments (Furman v. Georgia, 1972, p. 2727).

Two justices, Justice William Brennan and Justice Thurgood Marshall, held that capital punishment per se was unconstitutional. Justice William O. Douglas stated that the death penalty was unconstitutionally discriminatory because of its disproportionate impact on minority and lower-class individuals. Justices Potter Stewart and Byron White cited the "freakish and arbitrary manner in which the death penalty was imposed" as a problem (Furman v. Georgia, 1972, pp. 874–83). The majority ruled that the imposition of the death penalty was so arbitrary and capricious that it violated the Eighth Amendment.

At the time of this decision there were over 600 persons under death sentences in 32 states (Bedau, 1984). The Supreme Court reversed these death sentences in one multifaceted legislative act (Bedau, 1984). Although the ruling was not definitive, the decision invalidated the capital punishment laws of the federal government, the District of Columbia, and nearly all of the states that had retained the death penalty. None of the prisoners on death row at the time could be executed, nor could anyone be sentenced to death.

This ruling initiated what Zimring and Hawkins (1986) referred to as a *post-legislative frenzy.* Everywhere the public expressed fear that by ruling out the death penalty the Supreme Court was depriving citizens of lawful protection. People believed that with no death penalty more murders would be committed. Within two years, 28 states, including Oklahoma, had written new laws which, for the most part, responded to the Supreme Court's objections.

Although the Supreme Court voided the Oklahoma death penalty law on July 6, 1976, by July 24 of that same year, the Oklahoma legislature had drafted a new one. An article in the *Saturday Oklahoman & Times* dated July 10, 1976, stated, "Human lives could be at stake. The hiatus in capital punishment produced by the U.S. Supreme Court's voiding the Oklahoma statute means the perpetrators of murder in that period . . . will be given a license to kill" ("Capital Punishments," 1976).

Eventually the Supreme Court upheld the new laws of Georgia, Florida, Texas, and other states that had written specific guidelines for sentencing defendants to death. Some states, including Oklahoma, were sent back to the drawing boards to rewrite their laws. However, by 1977, executions were underway, and by the mid-1980s over 1,000 people were sentenced to death (Bedau, 1984). By 1985, a Gallup poll based on a sample of 1,523 adults indicated that 72 percent of Americans favored the death penalty for murder (Orlofsky, Bank, & Hitchings, 1985). As of February 1992, there were a total of 2,595 people under the sentence of death; the 45 women on death row make up 1.73 percent of this total (NAACP, 1992; *Facts on File*, 1992).

In a series of recent cases, the Supreme Court has been steadily closing the doors through which death-row inmates can petition the federal appeals courts to review their convictions. Currently, all nine justices, Souter, Blackmun, Kennedy, Thomas, Rehnquist, Stevens, White, O'Connor, and Scalia, though they are the final arbiters of justice, appear anxious to put full responsibility back into the hands of state lawmakers. This is not a new issue (Amsterdam, 1987), but given the climate of our times, it is very likely that the number of executions will continue to escalate.

A recent Supreme Court decision (May, 1992) ruled that federal courts are no longer obligated to grant a hearing on appeals by state prisoners even if the prisoners can show that their lawyers failed to present important facts in the trial. That means that any new or exonerating evidence may never be heard in court. This ruling weakens the habeas corpus law that has, until now, allowed death row inmates to appeal. Furthermore, this ruling may allow states to carry out executions more swiftly by avoiding the postponements of the appeals process.

WHY WOMEN COMMIT CAPITAL CRIMES

Undoubtedly, women kill for many of the same reasons that men do: out of anger, frustration, hatred, and, quite frequently, fear. Some women plan the murders they commit, and some commit them by accident. Some kill on the spur of the moment, in self-defense, or because there is a weapon at hand, and some kill while on drugs or alcohol. Some women kill because they are mentally ill.

According to data released in 1992 by the Georgia Department of Corrections, of the 235 women doing time for murder or manslaughter in Georgia, 44 percent killed a husband or lover (Hansen, 1992). Of these murders, 102 were classified as domestic killings. Forty-six women (almost half) claim that their partners beat them regularly, and 38 of these 46 had repeatedly reported domestic violence to the police.

In 1991, the U.S. Surgeon General listed domestic violence as the leading cause of injury to women: it was more prevalent than automobile accidents, rapes, and muggings combined. According to Schmittroth (1991), between 1,000 and 1,300 wives are killed by their husbands each year. In her book *When Battered Women Kill*, Dr. Angela Brown (1989) states that in this country, a woman's chances of being assaulted at home by her partner are greater than those of a police officer being assaulted on the job. Without intervention, domestic violence escalates, and occasionally, though still rarely, women strike back (Hansen, 1992; Trafford, 1991). When women do kill their intimate partners, they are given longer and more severe prison sentences than men. Women charged with homicide have the smallest number of prior arrests of all offenders (Bureau of Justice Statistics, 1988; PRRFIT, 1991; Schmittroth, 1991).

WOMEN ON DEATH ROW

The correctional system in this country warehouses its death row inmates (Johnson, 1980). Corrections people seem to believe, and perhaps rightly so, that if a woman is going to be executed, they should not spend a great deal of time on her comfort or rehabilitation. However, the reality is that women who are given the death penalty spend many long and isolated years on death row. Two of the 45 women currently on death row have been there for a decade (Bureau of Justice Statistics, 1989; PRRFIT, 1991).

A breakdown of the 45 women on death row indicates that 18 (40%) are statistically classified as black and 27 (60%) are classified as white. The 5 women in Oklahoma, whose ages range from 30 to 50, identify themselves as African American (1), Caucasian (3), and Native American (1). They are the mothers of 11 children and the grandmothers of several more (PRRFIT, 1991). They have all been convicted of murder or conspiracy to commit murder, and if they were executed in Oklahoma today, they would die by lethal injection.

Oklahoma's death row for women is located at Site 1, a maximum security women's prison that has double fences with double razor wires around its perimeter. The women are housed inside a locked and isolated unit, upstairs through a second locked glassed-in row of cells. Within this triply secured, isolated area, they are held in single locked cells for 23 out of 24 hours each day. It is a prison within a prison. They are not allowed to mingle with the general prison population or each other. They are put into a small locked outdoor exercise cage for an hour each day if the weather permits and if correctional officers have the time to escort and observe them. And, as one woman put it, "We are showered three times a week" (O'Shea, 1992). When they are moved from one area to another within the prison, they are handcuffed and shackled, and they are not allowed contact visits with family members. In their surveys, they speak of loneliness and isolation (PRRFIT, 1991). They spend their days coming to terms with what one woman has called an existential death. All of them mention a sense of emptiness and loss, and list being able to hug and kiss their children and have extended day visits with them as things they need the most (PRRFIT, 1991). One mother said, "Not just for us. . . .The children need it, too." In one woman's words, "It's loneliness, it's cruel, it's hell" (O'Shea, 1992).

The conditions under which the women on death row are held are undoubtedly a result of two prevalent concepts: the belief that women on death row represent a danger to other prisoners, and an underlying attitude that these women represent the worst of our society, and therefore, somehow, deserve to be isolated. Robert Johnson (1980), a death row criminologist who has worked with and studied men on death row, concluded that the lack of human contact causes death row inmates to lose their individual personality traits and experience what he calls a "death of the personality" that precedes their physical death (p. 547).

In contrast to the conditions under which women are kept, research points to some advances for men on death row. In an experiment conducted in a men's prison in Arkansas, it was discovered that when death row prisoners were allowed to mix with the general population and were given privileges for good behavior, they became model prisoners (Murton, 1969). A study by Sorenson and Marquart (1989) of work-capable death row inmates in Texas indicated that they were employed in a garment factory that set up its operations within a prison. The inmates who were employed reported that having to go to work every day gave them a reason to get up in the morning, and doing a job well gave them a sense of dignity.

Although a study comparing the conditions under which women are kept on death row with those of men has yet to appear, at least one conclusion can be drawn from what we know about men that is undoubtedly true for women: total isolation over long periods of time is dehumanizing.

In 1983, Coontz published a study of women who were sentenced to death and who were at that time awaiting their execution. Four of the women from among 13 on death row were interviewed in the summer of 1983. Coontz noted that the women's cells were of concrete block with a lavatory and sleeping provisions in each one, and that some had tables and chairs as well as lockers. These women reported spending 22 to 24 hours a day in their cells. They were all required to wear prison-issued clothing, and were not allowed to mingle with the general population. Coontz reported that although all of the women had their cases in appeals, none of them had a comprehensive understanding of the legal statutes, and none of them saw their lawyers more than once every few months.

Women on death row consistently express frustration about not understanding the judicial process. One woman stated that they could request law books from the library if they knew what they wanted, but since none of them knew anything about law, they didn't ask (O'Shea, 1992). She went on to explain that most of the women on death row do not have the background nor the education to understand what is in a law book even if they did get one. Another woman said that none of the women on death row understood the court system or the appeals process and that they had to rely totally on the information of one person: their court-appointed defender, who quite frequently believed they were guilty or did not like them (O'Shea, 1992).

Forcing women to sit idle for years in tiny cells, without normal human contact, contemplating their own execution creates physical as well as mental problems. Aside from an overwhelming sense of isolation, three of the women in our survey reported they had developed physical problems since their incarceration on death row. These problems included such things as high blood pressure, arthritis, and ulcers (PRRFIT, 1991).

Asked what might be of most benefit to herself and others, a woman on death row answered, "Jobs. . . . There's so much idle time. . . . We could get through it a lot better, even if it was sweeping the floor. . . . It would give you something to do instead of just emptiness" (O'Shea, 1992).

Death row inmates, especially women, are marginal members of our society economically as well as socially, and most of us, given the choice, would ignore them.

FUTURE DIRECTIONS FOR RESEARCH

Although a wealth of material exists in criminal justice literature on the subject of capital punishment and death row studies in reference to men, there is a paucity of materials that deal explicitly with women on death row. Some of the reasons for this are

1. Up to this point, the small numbers have not made women visible enough to be considered for study.
2. Since the criminal justice system is male oriented and run primarily by men, a study of the death penalty as it relates to women has not been considered important or relevant.
3. The strict security and isolation of women on death row have made them, for all practical purposes, inaccessible to researchers.

The literature that has appeared up to this point about women on death row has been in the context of the male experience or has dealt with individual women, such as the record Velma Barfield left of her experience on death row in the form of an autobiography entitled *Woman on Death Row* (1985).

In any consideration of women on death row, there are a number of intriguing questions still to be posed. A study needs to be done on death sentencing practices, specifically regarding women, and on how these practices may or may not discriminate against women. The issue of why women commit capital crimes begs for a detailed feminist perspective, and a thorough study of the conditions under which women are held as compared to those for men has yet to appear. Although some studies do exist about how mothers and families are affected by the prison experience (Barry, 1987; Baunach, 1982), we need to take a closer look at how having a mother on death row affects children and how being denied normal visiting privileges with their children affects the women themselves.

I have developed the following hypotheses that I will explore in future research:

1. For women, the death penalty is not a deterrent to violent crime. Most women who kill do so only once, and few, if any, have had previous criminal records.
2. Most women kill after a long history of abuse, and they usually kill the abuser, therefore, the death penalty seems extreme punishment for self-defense.
3. The manner in which the death penalty is handed down is gender biased, since similar crimes committed by men are not punished in like manner.
4. Since the death penalty for women today means long, painful, and isolated imprisonment without normal human contact, it may be considered another form of repression stemming from the economic hardships and other conditions of abuse experienced by women.

The findings of our studies seem to suggest that the imposition of the death penalty on women in this country is a male construct, both gender biased and oppressive, particularly in the South. Women's prisons hide their practices of oppression from society by keeping the women on death row invisible, thus stigmatizing and controlling them so that society, uncomfortable with the image conjured up by the words "death row," need not face its choices.

One hopes that future studies will shed more light on the effects of regionalism, racism, sexism, and other "isms" that discriminate against women in the practice of irrevocable punishments such as death.

TWO *The Institution*

In Part Two we examine the correctional system as it is today, looking at organizational perspectives, staff attitudes, communication, and relevant theories.

Beginning with Chapter 8, "Perspectives on Correctional Organizations," Dreama G. Moon, Beverly R. Fletcher, and Lynda Dixon Shaver take a look at organizational concepts and how they apply to prison organizations. Staff survey data from Sites 1 and 2 are utilized in this discussion.

In Chapter 9, " Attitudes of Correctional Staff," Chong Ho Yu and Susan Marcus-Mendoza scrutinize staff data from Sites 1 and 2.

Chapter 10, "The Relationship between Language Culture and Recidivism among Women Offenders," by Shaver, integrates the data from preliminary interviews and field observations to explore the communication phenomenon in the prison setting.

Throughout Chapter 11, "Toward an Integrated Theory of Female Criminality and Incarceration," Garry L. Rolison delves into various theories of female criminality, female imprisonment, and female recidivism. He critiques early as well as newer theories and notions.

With Chapter 12, Fletcher and Moon conclude the study in a summary manner, giving an overview of Parts 1 and 2 as well as predictions for the future.

"The strength is within all of us"

8   Perspectives on Correctional Organizations

Dreama G. Moon, Beverly R. Fletcher, and Lynda Dixon Shaver

This chapter examines the tenets of organizational communication analysis, organization development theories, and organization transformation theories in order to identify their usefulness and applicability within the context of prison organizations in general and Oklahoma women's prisons in particular.

One of the reasons for a multidisciplinary approach to the study of women offenders and recidivism is to utilize a variety of methods to investigate and thereby to understand correctional organizations. The communication perspective examines the organization as it exists through the language culture of its members (i.e., staff and inmates). Organization development and organization transformation provide specific means by which organizations are changed or transformed.

In this chapter, we examine some important questions: (1) How do prisons differ from other types of organizations? (2) What characteristics do prisons share with other types of organizations? (3) What aspects of organizational communication impact staff and inmates? (4) Is organization development theory useful in addressing the problems of prison organizations? (5) Is a more radical paradigm (i.e., organization transformation) needed? In addressing these questions, we draw upon sociological theory, organizational communication theories, and theories of organization development and organization transformation.

It is clear that prisons in the United States are not achieving their espoused goal of rehabilitating offenders. To see this, one has only to look at the rising recidivism rates and the ever-increasing numbers of correctional institutions, which continue to strain at the seams. In this chapter prisons are discussed in terms of characteristics common to other organizations as well as those unique to this particular organization type. The case is made that although organizational communications analyses and organization development interventions are useful for understanding the organization as it is, they are not sufficient by themselves to address the most serious problems faced by prison organizations in the United States. It may be that prisons are in need of radical change, that is, organization transformation.

ORGANIZATION PERSPECTIVE

Jablin, Putnam, Roberts, and Porter (1987) note that the study of organizations can be characterized by the following approaches: (1) classical (Taylor, 1911; Weber, 1947); (2) human relations (Lewin, 1947; Mayo, 1960; McGregor, 1960); (3) behavioral (Cyert & March, 1963; Simon, 1945); and (4) systems (Katz & Kahn, 1966). These approaches are primarily labeled as psychological approaches. They provide information for management control and implement interventions for organizational change and effectiveness. Organization development falls within the purview of this classification and contains all of the characteristics inherent in this description (i.e., classical, human relations, behavioral, and systems theories).

In contrast to the psychologically based perspective of the study of organizations are perspectives, labeled interpretive or symbolic, that focus on the social construction of reality (Billig et al., 1988; Blummer, 1969; Burke, 1966; Hummel, 1987; Mead, 1934; Putnam & Pacanowsky, 1983). Some researchers under this paradigm have analyzed organizations as cultures (Bolman & Deal, 1984; Burrell & Morgan, 1979; Pondy, et al. 1983; Sypher, Applegate, and Sypher, 1985). Both the communication perspective and the organization development perspective utilize cultural analyses in answering questions about organizational behavior.

Organization transformation is a perspective that defies classification. Covering all aspects of the organization, it is a new paradigm that looks at radical changes in the organization's beliefs, values, vision, mission, goals, cultural norms, structure, roles, communication processes, and its relationship to its environments, both internal and external (Fletcher, 1990).

ARE PRISONS ORGANIZATIONS?

The study of prisons as organizations has been relatively neglected. Although many individuals and groups in our society perceive prison organizations as ineffective, little methodical study into this assumption has occurred, and certainly few, if any, systematic plans for improving prison organizations have been developed. Part of the problem is that prisons are not often thought of as organizations, at least not in the sense that one thinks of more traditional organizations such as private businesses and public agencies. Prisons seem to be classified as "something else," although the exact nature of this "something else" has never been clearly defined.

In a study cited by Littlejohn (1989), Strother defines an *organization* as consisting "of two or more people involved in a cooperative relationship, which implies that they have collective goals. The members . . . differ in terms of function, and they maintain a hierarchal structure" (p. 225). Strother further recognizes that organizations exist within an environment that has impact on them. In light of this definition, it is clear that prisons (women's prisons in particular) are organizations that call for scrutiny and intervention.

Though it is clear that prisons meet the criteria that distinguish organizations from other kinds of entities, it is also clear that prisons are often conceptualized as being "something else," perhaps something more than what one generally imagines when one discusses more traditional types of organizations. In the literature, prisons have been conceptualized as organizations, total institutions, social systems, social organizations, and police states. Therefore, it is not surprising that this element of "something elseness" is difficult to define clearly. While it is true that prisons as organizations manifest the characteristics of organization (e.g., goals, policies, and procedures; hierarchal organization; composition of many people; and a life span exceeding that of a human lifetime), it is also true that prisons are miniature societies in which people both live and work. However, for the purposes of this chapter, we will focus our discussion on prisons as formal organizations and how they both resemble and differ from other types of organizations.

Structure

Structurally, as formal organizations, prisons have much in common with what we think of as more traditional organizations such as private businesses and governmental agencies. Prisons are typically organized in a bureaucratic fashion (Schrag, 1961; Williamson, 1990). This structure is viewed as enabling the equal treatment of inmates and inmate protection under due process standards required by law. It is also the result of administrative expediency (Williamson, 1990). Bureaucracy is characterized by: (1) a rules orientation and uniformly applied procedures, (2) a systematic and clearly defined division of labor, (3) hierarchy of authority, (4) employment of qualified personnel, (5) neutral competence as the criterion for advancement, (6) an impersonal environment, and (7) formal communication (Cressey, 1965; Cummings, Long, & Lewis, 1987; Schrag, 1961; Williamson, 1990).

Unlike other organizations, prisons manifest not one but three separate and distinct substructures or hierarchies: custodial, industrial, and professional or service (Cressey, 1965; Garrity, 1961). These substructures are not integrated by a common purpose, and each has its own objectives, roles, patterns of authority, communication channels, and so forth.

Environmental Impact

Like other organizations, prisons must be responsive to their environments in order to exist (Fletcher, 1990). In this sense, prisons are open systems (Williamson, 1990). Like other organizations, prisons must be responsive to a number of different constituents, the needs and desires of which may often be in conflict (Cressey, 1965; Williamson, 1990). Prisons must respond to the social environment (community), the political environment (legislators), the legal environment (courts), and the system environment (other parts of the criminal justice system). In addition to these external environments, prisons must also be responsive to their internal environments, which are comprised of both workers and residents (Cressey, 1965; Williamson, 1990).

Organizational Goals

Prisons, like other organizations, have stated goals. For prisons, these goals are usually articulated around issues of protection of the community (custody) and rehabilitation of the offender (treatment) (Garrity, 1961). The goals of prison organizations are often in conflict (Cressey, 1965; Galtung, 1961; Williamson, 1990). Galtung (1961) states that the central explanation for this is that the goals of custody and treatment embrace radically different ideologies. A custody orientation incorporates ideas such as: (1) crime results from exercise of individual free will and choice, (2) the function of prisons is to punish offenders, and (3) inmates should be dealt with uniformly and impersonally; a treatment orientation embraces ideas such as (1) criminal acts result from societal influences, (2) inmates are "sick" and in need of treatment, and (3) inmates should be dealt with in personal and individualized ways. Galtung goes on to say that a prison "organization that tries to maximize both goals will be ridden by internal conflicts" (pp. 123–24). Hepburn and Albonetti (1980) find that conflict among correctional staff is more likely to be a by-product of organizational goal conflicts than a by-product of the position of the staff in the organization.

Another characteristic of prisons is the extent to which their environment affects the development of organizational goals and subsequently related policies. Schrag (1961) states that "the objectives and policies of correctional institutions are largely reflections of beliefs and values that are indigenous to the broader community" (p. 331). If prison goals and policies deviate very far from those of the broader community, prison officials can expect to encounter various forms of public opposition as well as political and administrative pressure to conform. This reality perhaps constrains prisons much more than other organizations in the development of and change in their organizational goals. Moreover, public opinion, political pressure, and patriarchal values influence which organizational goals will take priority within the prison organization (Schrag, 1961).

Organizational Roles

Prisons, like other bureaucratic organizations, have a division of labor. However, a prison's dualistic nature and conflicting organizational substructures create a breeding ground for high levels of role conflict (Wheeler, 1961). Depending on whether one is employed in the custody or the treatment substructure, one will perceive one's role in the organization and the organization itself in very different ways (Cressey, 1965; Williamson, 1990). Moore (as cited in Kalinich & Pitcher, 1984) finds that job ambiguity was the highest job-related stressor reported by correctional staff. Due to the differing ideologies of custody and treatment goals, conflict may occur between organizational roles as well as within those roles.

Communication Systems

Prisons, similar to other organizations, have established communication channels; however, these channels tend to differ depending on whether the institution is orientated to custody or to treatment goals (Cressey, 1965; McCleery, 1961). Custody-oriented prisons tend to manifest communication systems reflective of other bureaucracies, that is, top-down communication, restricted communication between staff and staff and between staff and inmates, and use of formal channels for most communication. Treatment-oriented prisons tend to utilize more open-style communication systems, that is, extensive communication among staff and between staff and inmates is encouraged, communication flows in many directions, and informal channels are more highly utilized. Problems are inevitable in organizations that attempt to combine these very different approaches to communication. As McCleery (1961) observes, "The patterns of communication involved in a process of education and counseling are inconsistent with those required for authoritarian control" (p. 155).

Organizational Effectiveness

Prisons, like all other organizations, are concerned with meeting their stated goals. Unlike many other organizations, prison administrators are not free to organize and develop their institutions in ways they perceive as efficient or effective (Cressey, 1965). This is in part due to the influence and often contradictory ideas of outside interest groups, but it is also due to the conflict inherent in the incompatible goals and ideologies of custody and treatment substructures. Thus, the prison administrator often performs a balancing act between conflicting group interests and internal ideologies, which may or may not serve the best interests of the organization as a whole. Therefore, change in prisons tends to be reactionary rather than planned. Administrators tend to respond to "whoever screams the loudest," in the interest of their own administrative survival (Cressey, 1965). Cressey goes on to say that "new services and roles are added without regard to existing ones . . . and are organized around purposes little related to one another" (p. 1024).

Authority

Although there is a clear chain of formal command within prison organizations, the manifestations of authority are somewhat different from those in most organizations. In prisons, a much broader array of conduct is subject to authority (including staff dress, deportment, and manners), and such matters constantly come up for judgment (Goffman, 1961). Many prisons have policies that require staff to monitor one another in these areas and to provide written reports of violations to their supervisors. Correctional officers are unique in that they have no counterpart in the "real" world—each is at the same time a worker and a manager due to his or her supervision of inmates. The prison is one type of organization wherein management is an end rather than a means (Cressey, 1965).

Control

Another unique characteristic of prison organizations is the primacy of focus on security or control (Schrag, 1961). Day-to-day activities are predictable and highly routinized, with very little deviation (Galtung, 1961). Furthermore, staff spend a great deal of their day administering a carefully constructed system of privileges and punishments as well as performing many rote activities, such as locking and unlocking doors, counting heads, escorting inmates to various locations, and so on (Goffman, 1961b). The next section examines the communications perspective of cultural analyses.

THE COMMUNICATION PERSPECTIVE IN CORRECTIONS

One learns about processes at work in an organization by examining the specific language culture and behaviors of the organization's members. Billing and colleagues (1988), Hummel (1987), and Burke (1966) say that researchers can access the conflicts in organizations through analyses of the language of the members of the organization. Analysis from the communication perspective seems necessary as a part of the initial stages of an organizational change project. Communication techniques are useful as ongoing meta-analyses of the organization in conjunction with practices that focus more directly on changing the organization, such as organization development and organization transformation. This section posits that a study focusing on the language of an organization implies that the members have a language culture that is created through and perpetuated by the organization's members. For corrections, this is a bureaucratic correctional language that serves to set roles for its members, establish behavior for interaction, and control the allocation of resources of the organization for staff and inmates.

Analysis of Site 1

The communication analysis of Site 1 is based on ethnographic data from the site and interviews with the members of the organization in order to determine the dilemmas involved in the interaction among the various members of the organization.

A traditional study of an organization would label the institution as a part of a large state governmental bureaucracy—the Oklahoma Department of Corrections. The characteristics of bureaucracies (i.e., fixed job positions, dehumanized decisions, machinelike organizational patterns, and so forth) have been well documented in studies conducted through the years (Blau, 1974, 1955; Weber, 1947). These studies have focused on both the functions and the structures of such organizations (Blau, 1981; Durkheim, 1964). The fixed structure of bureaucracies and the avowed purposes of the organization are easily accessed through organizational charts and mission statements. In contrast to previous studies, the purpose of this analysis is to look at the day-to-day interactions and to learn from that process.

The Oklahoma Department of Corrections (DOC) and Site 1 are typical of governmental agencies and bureaucracies in structure and function. A broader and deeper understanding of the major sources of conflict within this organization can be assessed through: (1) participant observation and field notes, (2) interviews, and (3) open-ended response surveys. The language culture analysis utilized in the interview and survey analyses is discussed in more detail in Chapter 10. From these qualitative methodologies come insights into the language culture of this organization—a culture created and perpetuated by the interaction of its members.

Organizational talk is not unique to corrections. In previous research, Glenn (1990) noted that in a health care facility that provides bureaucratic therapy, the interaction between a doctor and her or his patients could be analyzed in terms of certain organizing features. That is, the status differences, the roles of the participants, and the purpose of the doctor-patient visit combined to create stages within the interaction that revealed the unequal control of the participants. Analysis of organizational talk at Site 1 reveals similar organizing features. This similarity indicates that much of the interaction between members of organizations is not interpersonal communication representing the individual; rather, the individual is speaking "organizational speech." The person adopts the language culture of the organization and adapts to the perspective of the organization. Hummel (1987) notes that bureaucratic language is

specifically designed to insulate functionaries from clients, to empower them not to have to listen, unless the client first learns the language. For the client who has learned the language is a client who has accepted the bureaucrat's values. Language defines both what problems we can conceive of and what solutions we can think of. (p. 181)

The adaptation of both staff and, ultimately, some inmates results in perspectives of the members that are single-mindedly committed to the good of the organization. That "good of the organization," ironically, may not be also the "good of the client" (i.e., the inmate).

The organizational culture at Site 1, as with all multilevel organizations, has developed over time under the influence of the parent organization (the DOC). The activities of the staff and their responses to inmates have remained essentially the same through the years in women's institutions. A superficial analysis would suggest that women's prisons are now more sophisticated and have very different missions than in earlier times. In reality, the purposes of correctional institutions have not changed. Their implicit mission (which often differs from the stated mission) has been to isolate criminals from society and to cope with the problems inherent with that mission. Essentially, the tasks of staff are to (1) organize the inmates according to their crimes; (2) provide the basic essentials of human life for inmates with varying degrees of outsider-perceived humanity; (3) develop programs of activity for the inmates as pressured to do so by the DOC, society, and, to a lesser degree, reactions of the inmates; and (4) adapt the daily schedules of the inmates to the needs of the organization.

Conflicts in the Organization

In any bureaucracy, the self-description of the bureaucracy is generally the source of wry humor and self-depreciation by its members. Staff, with humor, point out the problems in working for a system that doesn't respond to individual needs. The inmates complain that all of their needs take too long to be met because of "bureaucracy."

An analysis of the perspectives of both staff and inmates reveal dilemmas involved in their dealings with one another. The staff assumes that the supervisors who are in charge are able to be responsive to their individual needs. Staff members, regardless of their level of adherence to the system, continually push against the restraints of bureaucratic inflexibility to find room for individual attention to their own personal needs. The irony of such complaints is that these staff members will answer inmate complaints with the same inflexibility that they face from their own supervisors. The indoctrination of staff to the system and their adaptation of bureaucratic language ensures that the inmates will face the same impersonal responses to their individual needs. This adaptation to the system by staff is assured by the socialization process that is done on both a formal basis (i.e., initial department-wide training and on-site training, as well as yearly training thereafter) and an informal basis.

The staff functions as "front-line warriors" to protect Site 1's resources. The organization maintains the status quo and perpetuates itself through the control of those resources. Resources include finite physical supplies, such as sanitary napkins and toilet paper, and nonfinite supplies such as the degree of association or socialization with staff. The very act of restricting these resources further encourages the employee to adopt the organizational perspective. Certain inmates (e.g., trustees or longtime residents) are also, by the nature of their duties, encouraged to adopt the organizational perspective and to take part in the restriction of resources to other inmates.

The inmates are also given on-site orientation or training. They, too, are socialized by staff (formally and informally) and by other inmates (informally). As will be discussed in Chapter 10, the adaptation or refusal/failure of the inmate to adapt to the organization's perspective has several long-term implications for those inmates. Inmates enter the system with varying degrees of expectations. With little or no previous information, the first-time offender will often have unrealistic (from the organization's perspective) expectations. The conflicts between this person and staff usually result in the "correct" adaptation by the inmate to fit into the system.

Repeat offenders have very clear understandings of what the system will and will not do. The adaptation of these offenders can be characterized in terms of learning the system and having "realistic" expectations. The negative aspect of this adaptation is that the person becomes accustomed to the workings of the organization and upon release is often uncomfortable with the system of "the street," which is unorganized, unpredictable, ambiguous, and responsive in unexpected ways. In a way in which the organization does not intend, adaptation to the prison system can result in "model" inmates who are unable to adjust to the outside culture. This is particularly true with regard to long-term inmates or inmates who are frequent recidivists.

What, then, are the primary conflicts at Site 1? The employees have information about their organization and how it functions, yet they (the staff) retain the notion that they will be treated as individuals. Staff people persist in the concept of individual employee treatment despite the fact that the organization is designed for and dedicated to aggregate treatment of both employees and inmates. Because expectations are rarely met, a negative climate or interaction results.

In interaction with inmates, employees use bureaucratic organizational speech. The organization sustains its resources and its use of the resources through staff members. The role of the staff is most clearly revealed in this "front-line warrior" position.

The inmate, whether new or returning, is subjected to organizational speech by the staff and by other inmates. The incarcerated individual's choices are (1) to adapt and become a model prisoner, or (2) not to adapt, becoming a "difficult" prisoner. Many inmates embrace the organizational perspectives and the bureaucratic language and adapt to the predictable nature of prison. Upon release, these inmates find themselves ill prepared to deal with a less than predictable world.

In sum, correctional systems, historically, have been governmental bureaucracies that are subject to established perspectives involving inherent dilemmas in the interactions between staff and the organization and between the staff/organization and inmates. Correctional systems have sought to respond to societal pressure and, to a lesser degree, inmate pressure to change the organization in order to meet the needs of inmates. The privatization of prisons is one such response in recent times. Analysis of discussions with employees of private prison systems suggests that privatization has not changed the organizational culture of corrections. Rather, privatization has adopted the model of governmental bureaucratic correctional systems. In previous research, Glenn (1990) suggests that the organizational culture of bureaucracies persists through changes in sites, administration changes, and the contracting of care to outsider groups.

The implications of these findings suggest that research from a communication perspective is useful in confirming the stability of the organizational culture. Further, correctional organizations could use these findings to understand the dilemmas involved in forcing inmates to conform to the organizational culture and the relationship of conformity to recidivism. Further, communication meta-analysis of interactants and the organization should accompany the implementation of change programs developed to address recidivism.

THE ORGANIZATION DEVELOPMENT PERSPECTIVE

As a discipline, organization development is aimed at assisting organizations in identifying and rectifying obstacles to meeting the stated goals of organizations. It involves planned change. It seems peculiar that this field of knowledge has not been used in the context of prisons, which, according to prison administrators, staff, and inmates as well as the community at large have historically been unsuccessful in achieving the various goals they espouse.

Cummings and Huse (1989, p. 538) define *organization development* (OD) as "a system-wide effort applying behavioral science knowledge to the planned creation and reinforcement of organizational strategies, structures, and processes for improving an organization's effectiveness." In OD, the focal point is on improving the organization's ability to assess and resolve its own problems (Cummings and Huse, 1989). OD assumes that effective organizations are able to solve their own problems and that they have a high quality of work life and high productivity.

As an approach to organizational change, OD contains several features that differentiate it from other approaches. First, OD is based on behavioral science knowledge and practice, which addresses the personal and social needs in organizations as well as the rational and technical aspects of organizations. Second, although OD is concerned with planned change, it is a more flexible approach than the typical rigid and formalized approaches usually associated with business planning. Third, OD is not only concerned with creating change, it also includes the institutionalization of the change. Fourth, OD encompasses change on many levels—structure, strategy, and process (communication). Finally, OD is aimed at improving organizational effectiveness (Cummings and Huse, 1989).

OD evolved from four major backgrounds: (1) the development of training groups (T-groups) and the growth of the National Training Laboratories, (2) early work in survey research and feedback, (3) action research as related to planning and managing change, and (4) the approach focusing on productivity and quality of work life (Cummings and Huse, 1989). From these beginnings, many different approaches to OD have developed: so too, have conceptualizations of organizations. Bolman and Deal (1984) have identified four major views of organizations: (1) organizations as rational systems, (2) organizations as human resource systems, (3) organizations as political arenas, and (4) organizations as cultures.

In the rational systems view, organizational structure (goals, roles, and technology) is emphasized. The goal is to develop these structures in such a way as to best fit the organizational purpose and meet the demands of the environment. In the human resource systems perspective, the focus is on the interdependence between people and organizations. Here the end is to best fit people's needs, skills, and values into the formal roles and relationships necessary to accomplish organizational goals. Power, conflict, and the allocation of scarce resources in organizations are the foci of the political arena view. Strategies for effectively managing organizational power and conflict are stressed. In the last perspective, the focus is on the problems of meaning in organizations. This view rejects the assumption that organizations are rational entities.

THE ORGANIZATION TRANSFORMATION PERSPECTIVE

Organization transformation (OT) evolved out of organization development to fill a need that was not met in OD theory, namely, a threat to the entire organizational system. The majority of OT theorists advocate a holistic systems perspective, which includes more environmental variables than usual systems models. Buckley and Perkins (as cited in Fletcher, 1990, p. 4) refer to this as a "holistic–ecological systems perspective," which emphasizes the fundamental interdependence and interrelatedness of all phenomena. They maintain that this new perspective involves a *paradigm shift*, defined as a "profound change in the thoughts, values, and perceptions that form a particular vision of reality" (p. 4). Fletcher (1990) defines *organization transformation* as:

an ecological, holistic approach to radical, revolutionary, second-order change in the entire context of the organization's system from a humanistic perspective. This involves transformative changes in the fundamental nature of the organization and requires completely new ways of thinking, behaving, and perceiving by members of the organization. OT strategies help the organization to be flexible and responsive to internal and external environments. OT strategies transform the organization's vision and mission. (p. 149)

Cummings and Huse (1989) state that OT is "a process of radically altering the organization's strategic direction, including fundamental changes in structures, processes, and behaviors" (p. 539). Organization development is aimed at detecting and correcting deviations from the organization's stated vision, mission, and goals, while organization transformation is directed at transforming the organization's vision, mission, and goals. Wilbur (as cited in Adams, 1984, p. vii) likens OD to "moving the furniture around" within a room, while OT is like "moving the furniture to a new floor." Skibbins (as cited in Fletcher, 1990) describes the process of transformation as radical change. He defines radical change as "a large-scale, high-speed process that occurs within a single entity, a process analogous to that which occurs in caterpillars metamorphosing into butterflies, mycelia into mushrooms, and tadpoles into frogs" (p. 6). Thus, the thing becomes something totally different. Furthermore, Skibbins sees radical organization change as continuous—a sort of infinite metamorphosis.

Harman (1988) and Fletcher (1990) view OT as a systemwide process requiring all organization members to perceive, think, value, and behave in completely new ways. In the words of Owen (1987, p. 10), it involves creating a "new story" of the organization that radically erases old perceptions and behaviors. Tushman, Newman, and Nadler (as cited in Fletcher, 1990) describe OT as "discontinuous and frame-breaking change" that involves "sharp, simultaneous changes in controls, power, strategy, and structure" (p. 8).

Adams (1984, p. ix) identifies six themes present in OT: (1) vision, (2) new perspectives, (3) organization as an energy field, (4) leadership, (5) performance excellence, and (6) human empowerment. Vision indicates the importance of clarifying the goals and purposes of the organization and emphasizes the importance of agreement with the vision and commitment to it. New perspectives necessitate the questioning of previously taken-for-granted basic organizational assumptions and beliefs. It calls for new ways of knowing that are more holistic, expansive, and relativistic. Organization as an energy field is a term used by Adams to describe the powerful impact of organizational culture. The components of culture are the collective traditions, myths, and beliefs of the organization. Leadership is seen as playing a crucial role in creating and sustaining the vision, encouraging support of the vision, and inspiring learning, exploration, and creativity. Performance excellence, the extremely competent execution and completion of required or desired tasks on all levels of the organization, is viewed as of the utmost importance. Human empowerment involves creating an environment that encourages organization members to work toward achieving their potentials. This theme focuses on individual well-being and on encouraging self-responsibility, the modification of self-limiting beliefs, and the development of the spiritual self (Adams, 1984).

Fletcher (1992) has made seven additions to the six themes: (1) coming to terms with chaos, (2) providing open space, (3) practicing radical authenticity, (4) realizing connectedness, (5) releasing blame, (6) taking responsibility, and (7) accepting.

Coming to terms with chaos is required when organizations face crisis, threat, and confrontation. In chaos, there is extreme discomfort and emotions run wild. To come to terms with chaos, organizations must be able to reframe the chaos into opportunity. Open space is the space in which transformation occurs. It tends to occur naturally during chaos and can be greatly facilitated by a change agent who understands the process. It involves removing old structures, letting go and taking risks, believing in the process, and creating, conceiving, and birthing the new organization. Radical authenticity involves self-disclosure, giving and receiving constructive feedback or criticism. Realizing connectedness involves a positive premise about people and unconditional positive regard. Paradoxically, we must be able to appreciate and value our differences before we are able to realize our fundamental connectedness. Releasing blame is simply forgiving. Forgiving is an internal process that involves the release of "self blame" and the release of "other blame." Releasing blame causes inner peace and enables individuals to understand their essential connection to other people. Taking responsibility requires that individuals realize their role and power as change agents. It also involves empowering other people to be responsible by sharing power and providing open space. This involves encouraging, acknowledging, and rewarding positive risk-taking behaviors. And finally, accepting has to do with receiving and acknowledging the new organizational form. This is a process that doesn't just happen because we want it to—it involves grief work. It involves the dying of the old organization and the birthing of the new. In this process, the organization collectively grieves its passing in a manner similar to an individual—it goes through shock, denial, bargaining, anger, guilt, and finally acceptance. So the process involves mourning the death of the old; envisioning, creating, and birthing the new; celebrating the new birth; and finally accepting the new organization.

COMPARISON AND CONTRAST OF OD AND OT THEORIES

Communication theories are subsumed under organization development theory and have an integral place in OD analyses and strategies. In order to fully comprehend the essential, though sometimes subtle, differences between OD and OT approaches, it is useful to examine some of the characteristics that distinguish them from one another.

Some authors suggest that it is useful to distinguish between what is meant by the terms *change* and *transformation*. Perkins and Buckley (as cited in Fletcher, 1990) explain that while change deals with the modification of behaviors, beliefs, and attitudes, transformation is a "profound fundamental change in action and thought involving an irreversible discontinuity in the status quo" (p. 8).

Another useful way to conceptualize the difference between OD and OT is to examine two types of change that may occur within organizations: first order and second order. In first-order change (OD), a subunit of an organization may change without substantially affecting the nature of the organization as a whole. This type of change would include relatively minor and often naturally occurring improvements and adjustments that do not affect the organization's core nature or require a shift in perception. Second-order change (OT) is defined by Levy and Merry (1986, p. 5), as a "multi-dimensional, multi-level, qualitative, discontinuous, radical organizational change involving a paradigmatic shift."

It is imperative to note that OD and OT do not represent polarities; one is not "better" than the other. Each is useful within particular contexts. Indeed, a comprehensive OT effort would necessarily include OD techniques and strategies. The main difference seems to be in the focal point of each. OD seeks to improve on what is in an organization, while OT seeks to change the very nature of what is there. Where OD focuses on issues of effectiveness within the parameters of an organization's stated purpose, OT focuses on changing the purpose itself (Fletcher, 1990).

SUMMARY

The literature on prison organizations illustrates the special problems that they pose to those who work in them. It is also clear that prisons as organizations present special challenges to the concepts of organizational change. Incredibly, prisons have remained substantially unchanged for the last 70 years. One reason is that public sentiment about prisons is characterized by ambivalence and ignorance. Prisons are shrouded in secrecy and seen as necessary evils better left ignored. If prisons are thought of at all, it is generally in crisis situations, and then the focus is usually on security considerations (Baker, 1985; Galtung, 1961).

The presence of prisons in our society is ignored by the general public and academe. In academe, prisons have been viewed as the problem of sociologists when considered at all (Goffman, 1961b). Theory and research about prisons from other disciplinary perspectives, such as history, communication, human relations, psychology, anthropology and organization theory, are lacking. Attention and expertise from these other disciplines is needed if prisons are to become effective as organizations (Moon, 1991).

It is the position of the authors that a "new story" about prisons is needed. There appears to be general agreement that prisons as currently conceived are not serving their intended function and are ineffective organizations. Rapidly increasing prison populations, overcrowding, high rates of recidivism, and a general lack of solutions for improvement attest to the state of crisis that prisons are in. Furthermore, these complex problems may be insolvable unless prisons themselves undergo major transformation. The unique characteristics and inherent structural problems of prisons call for a radical approach; the old solutions are no longer working. Prisons need to be examined with a fresh eye—one that looks at prisons as they could be rather than as they are.

Due to its broadness of scope and radical nature, organization transformation theory may offer a new approach to the reconstruction of prisons as more effective organizations. It is suggested that it is the nature of prison organizations that needs to be addressed. Whether or not prisoners are rehabilitated, they are usually released when their time has been served. If prisons are to meet their goal of rehabilitation, then, clearly, a radically new approach is needed.

9 Attitudes of Correctional Staff

Chong Ho Yu and Susan Marcus-Mendoza

The final phase of our research project involves designing programs for inmates that will enable them to successfully adjust to life outside of prison, thereby reducing recidivism. Programs to educate staff about the experience of women in prison and to train staff to assist inmates in their readjustment may be important to achieving this goal. To understand the impact of staff attitudes on inmates, we must first determine what the attitudes of staff are and how they differ among staff members. The focus of this chapter is to examine the attitudes of the staff in Site 1 and Site 2 prisons regarding the purpose of corrections and to look at factors that are related to those attitudes.

THE PURPOSE OF CORRECTIONS

According to the President's Commission on Law Enforcement and Administration of Justice, theories regarding the purposes of corrections are extremely diverse (cited in Hartinger, Eldefonso, & Coffey, 1973). However, these theories can be categorized into five major viewpoints: (1) signifier, (2) retribution, (3) general deterrence, (4) special deterrence, and (5) rehabilitation.

Those who perceive that it is the purpose of corrections to be a *signifier* of the law are uninterested in whether or not lawbreakers committed immoral behaviors and deserve punishment. They believe lawbreakers must be punished just because laws exist and have been broken. Newman (1978) states that punishment "signifies to the actor and audience that there is a rule and it has been broken. . . . The sentence is the commandment, and the commandment is the punishment" (p. 8). This view is shared by

Rawls (1971), who posits "the principle of fair play," or "justice as fairness." Rawls contends that some "misconduct," such as speeding, might not do any harm to society; however, citizens still have a moral obligation to obey the law. Fairness stipulates that all citizens should obey the law.

The belief that a prison sentence is punishment for committing a crime, or *retribution*, is more popular than the preceding perspective. Middendorff (1971) assets that "throughout the history of civilization, retribution was the most widely prevalent and continuously persistent goal of punishment. It continues to be a major ingredient of the present systems of penal law in all parts of the world" (p. 11).

Some penologists use retribution and reprobation interchangeably. *Reprobation* implies a strong sense of condemnation, resentment, and disapproval of criminal behavior. Currently, most criminologists and correctional workers prefer the term retribution to reprobation.

Retribution is also different from revenge. *Revenge* suggests taking the law into one's own hands rather than allowing the justice system to preside over the distribution of consequences. As a result, the punishment may not be proportionate to the crime committed. Retribution, on the other hand, equates punishment with the crime committed and is imposed by a law enforcement agency. Punishing war criminals 40 years after the fall of the Nazi regime is an example of retribution. It probably serves no deterrent function, but it imposes punishment on the criminals (Nettler, 1982).

Others maintain that retribution is desirable since only through painful punishment can criminals purge their sins. Atonement through suffering has been a major theme in religious thought through the ages, and it still plays a role in thought about secular punishment (Packer, 1971).

Grupp (1971) stated that retribution must be viewed within the cultural context. Punishment and its interpretation varies from time to time and from place to place. What is viewed as punitive today may have been viewed differently at another time in history. For example, today sustained solitary confinement is seen as inhumane punishment, but in 1800 isolation was considered a means for rehabilitation and a way for the criminals to reconcile with God.

The third and fourth views of the purpose of corrections are types of *deterrence*. The notion of prison as a means of deterrence is based upon utilitarianism. The good that is thought to result from punishing criminals is the prevention or reduction of a greater evil (Packer, 1971). General deterrence, also known as *incapacitation*, hinders the criminals from doing more harm to society by physically separating them from others or disabling them (through execution, mutilation, exile, or banishment).

Currently, in the United States incarceration is the most prevalent means of general deterrence. *Special* or *secondary deterrence* places the emphasis on potential offenders. Punishment of offenders sets an example for other citizens of what will happen if the law is broken, and thus law-abiding behaviors are promoted.

Lastly, some psychologists, such as Karl Menninger (1969), favor *rehabilitation*, or *reformation*. Stanley Grupp (1971) defined rehabilitation as "the individualization of punishment and working with the individual in such a way that he [she] will be able to make a satisfactory adjustment, or at least a non-criminal adjustment, once he [she] is released from the authority of the state" (p. 8). However, some people perceive rehabilitation as a kind of experiment with involuntary subjects. Wolf Middendorff (1971) commented that rehabilitation can be very inhumane because inmates become guinea pigs of psychiatrists and psychologists. We believe that rehabilitation, or the opportunity for self-improvement and for inmates to optimize their chances of making a successful adjustment to life after prison, has to be one of the purposes of corrections if recidivism is to be reduced.

CURRENT STUDY

A total of 147 staff members at two prisons for women in Oklahoma responded to the survey, which was administered to small groups of inmates by two or more members of the research team. Demographic information about these staff members is presented in Table 9.1

Information on attitudes about corrections is presented in Table 9.2. Based on the answers given to question 32, "What do you think the purpose of 'corrections' is?", we coded the responses using the following five categories: (1) retribution, (2) general deterrence, (3) special deterrence, (4) rehabilitation, and (5) signifier. After coding all the responses, we adopted the following coding scheme:

1. general and special deterrence
2. rehabilitation
3. general and special deterrence and rehabilitation

Other viewpoints on corrections were not sufficiently represented to be included in the analyses.

Data from Site 1 and 2 were examined separately, and then combined to create one data set after determining by chi-square analysis that no significant difference existed between the two groups of correctional

Table 9.1			
Demographics of Staff Members			
		Site 1	Site 2
Number of Staff	Male	37.7%	58.8%
	Female	62.3%	41.2%
Mean Age		40.39%	37.32%
Marital Status	Widowed	-----	3.4%
	Single	11.5%	8.0%
	Common Law	-----	1.1%
	Married	68.9%	67.8%
	Divorced	18.0%	17.2%
	Separated	1.6%	2.3%
Race	Black	16.2%	21.6%
	White	61.8%	53.6%
	Others	22.1%	24.7%
Education	Below High School	1.6%	0.5%
	High School	42.2%	45.5%
	College	37.5%	46.0%
	Graduate School	18.7%	7.9%

workers on the question of the purpose of corrections. Chi-squares were used for all analyses since our data was categorical. Table 9.2 indicates the percentage of responses about the purpose of corrections given by staff members at Site 1 and Site 2.

More staff members involved with treatment included both rehabilitation and deterrence in their conception of corrections (50% versus 16.95%), whereas staff members involved with corrections tended to specify only deterrence or corrections in their responses. By collapsing response categories, it is evident that more of the staff members whose jobs are related to treatment included both rehabilitation (66.67% versus 61.02%) and deterrence (88.33% compared to 53.93%) in their definition.

Additionally, we examined whether or not being born in Oklahoma as opposed to any other state in the United States was related to the view of the purpose of corrections. The chi-square was significant (10.248, $p = 0.006$), and the phi coefficient was 0.273. Frequencies are presented in Table 9.2

While those born in Oklahoma were fairly evenly divided as to their concept of corrections, most individuals born outside Oklahoma (57.14%) stated that rehabilitation was the purpose of corrections. Overall, 61.5% of staff members who were born in Oklahoma, compared to 85.71% of group 2 staff members born outside Oklahoma, included rehabilitation in their definition.

Table 9.2		
Percentage of Responses about the Purpose of Corrections by Prison, Job Type, and Place of Birth		
BY PRISON:	<u>Site 1</u>	<u>Site 2</u>
1. General and special deterrence	33.3%	28.6%
2. Rehabilitation	30.2%	46.4%
3. General and special deterrence and rehabilitation	36.5%	25.0%
BY JOB TYPE:	<u>Treatment</u>	<u>Corrections</u>
1. General and special deterrence	33.33%	38.98%
2. Rehabilitation	16.17%	44.07%
3. General and special deterrence and rehabilitation	50.00%	16.95%
BY PLACE OF BIRTH:	Born in <u>Oklahoma</u>	Born outside <u>Oklahoma</u>
1. General and special deterrence	37.5%	14.29%
2. Rehabilitation	31.25%	57.14%
3. General and special deterrence	31.25%	28.57
N	96	42

A chi-square analysis of the relation between job category and place of birth was not significant. Therefore, there does not seem to be an interaction between these two variables.

We also conducted analyses to determine whether sex, race, education, history of abuse, marital status, and job satisfaction were related to staff's conceptualization of the objective of corrections. No significant results were obtained.

DISCUSSION

To further our understanding of the attitudes of correctional staff, we examined their attitudes toward the purpose of corrections and the factors that might be correlated to these attitudes. This study found that job category and whether or not the staff member was born in Oklahoma were related to the staff member's opinion of the purpose of corrections. These two variables were not correlated.

It is not surprising to find that more individuals in the psychological, educational, and medical services (group 1) saw the purpose of corrections as rehabilitation than individuals in the custodial (correctional officers') jobs. Since the goals of these professions include helping individuals to improve themselves in some way, it is reasonable that staff who work in these professions would see part of their task as rehabilitation. In addition, training in all of these professions includes skills for effective helping. However, correctional staff, who were less likely to perceive the purpose of corrections to be rehabilitation, are not usually formally trained to be effective helpers. More research would be needed to ascertain why staff members in group 1 defined the purpose of corrections as being both deterrence and rehabilitation.

Studies also suggest that most prison officers do not choose this profession because they desire to help inmates. Kauffman (1988) studied 40 officer recruits in the Massachusetts prison system to examine motivation for becoming a prison officer. When asked about their primary motivation, 53 percent cited economic reasons (most had recently been or were about to be laid off from their jobs). Twenty percent stated they wanted to be law officers, and two recruits expressed hostility toward inmates and saw themselves as "society's avengers" (p. 174). Only 28 percent stated their primary motivation to be a desire to help inmates.

Our study does not address the temporal relationship between attitude and profession. It is impossible to say whether staff who work in education, psychology, and medical fields entered these professions with the attitude that rehabilitation is an important part of corrections or, alternatively, their subsequent training and/or work in the prison field fostered this attitude. However, our study failed to find a significant relation between the attitude that rehabilitation is the purpose of corrections and education in general. Therefore, it seems that level of education is not a significant factor, but the type of education received might be important. Staff members who are trained in working with others to promote self-improvement might be more effective in working with inmates. Therefore, an important component of a program aimed at reducing recidivism might be staff training in helping skills.

Next, the relation between place of birth and attitude about the purpose of corrections was examined. As reported, we found that only 61.5 percent of Oklahomans compared to 85.71 percent of staff members born outside Oklahoma included rehabilitation in their definition. This does not appear to be related to our other significant variable, job category. While we do not know if all those individuals who were born in Oklahoma and are currently working in one of these two prisons have spent all or most of their lives in Oklahoma, we feel safe in assuming that a good portion of them have lived in Oklahoma continuously. It is impossible at this point in our study to speculate as to why people born in this state are less likely to include rehabilitation in their definition of corrections. However, the finding does suggest that other factors unrelated to the women who are incarcerated may be important in discovering why more women per capita are incarcerated in Oklahoma than in any other state.

Our findings suggest several areas for further research. First, it would be useful to know more about the relation between the attitudes of staff and their ability to work with and train inmates in the necessary skills to adjust successfully to life outside prison. Second, it would be useful to know how and when staff members develop their attitudes toward corrections. Do they adopt them early in life, and if so, is there something about the experience of living in Oklahoma that makes them less likely than those from other states to think that rehabilitation is important? Do these attitudes also permeate the justice system in Oklahoma, making it more likely that female offenders will be "deterred" than "rehabilitated"? Third, it would also be important to examine whether, regardless of how staff members' attitudes are formed, their attitudes toward corrections could be changed through education, and if so, what kind of education might be most effective? Whatever direction research takes, it seems important to further examine these areas in order to understand the prison experience of women in Oklahoma and to further our goal of reducing recidivism.

10 The Relationship between Language Culture and Recidivism among Women Offenders

Lynda Dixon Shaver

This chapter on women offenders and the correctional organization at Site 1 is based on an analysis of the language culture of the members of this correctional organization. The analysis explores major dilemmas that create the perspectives of both inmates and staff. These perspectives provide insight into the rising rates of recidivism among women offenders in Oklahoma. The analysis is accomplished by focusing on the "what" and the "how" of the language culture; that is, the words of staff and inmates are analyzed for their perspectives by examining what was said and how it was said. Inmate and staff perceptions about self, the correctional organization, inmates, staff, purposes of corrections, and reasons for recidivism were revealed by written responses in our inmate and staff surveys administered at Site 1 and in preliminary audiotaped interviews.

LANGUAGE CULTURE ANALYSIS

Communication is defined in diverse ways, including segmentation into categories such as verbal and nonverbal. *Verbal* refers to spoken and written communication. *Nonverbal* is defined as gesticulation, proxemics, olfactics, architecture, and so forth. In reality, communication is the culture of humans, and the whole of human behavior is communication (Hall, 1966). Analyses of communication are accomplished through a variety of methods, and the purpose of all such analyses is to better understand human interaction and behavior.

Language culture analysis suggests that the study of organizations is the study of the language and the culture of the organizational members (Billig et al., 1988; Hummel, 1987; Ricoeur, 1991; Shaver & Shaver, 1992). Such analysis is supported by research in many disciplines, including communication, sociology, cultural anthropology, and psychology (Atkinson & Heritage, 1984; Frankel, 1984; Geertz, 1973; Goffman, 1961a; Moreman, 1988; Potter & Wetherell, 1987; Putnam & Pacanowsky, 1983; Rabinow & Sullivan, 1979; Werth, 1981).

Billig and colleagues (1988) demonstrate that the language of members of an organization can be analyzed to access dilemmas that are the sites of conflict in the organization. The analysis can be of both written and oral language, such as the written responses from our surveys and our preliminary audiotaped interviews. This analysis identifies the language culture of the correctional bureaucracy and posits that language culture analysis is a method that can access the major dilemmas among inmates and staff in a prison for women. Furthermore, the analysis provides insights into the reasons for the increasing rate of recidivism among incarcerated women.

Language was analyzed by attention to what was said and how the speaker said the "what." Perceptions about self, the correctional organization, inmates, staff, purposes of corrections, and reasons for recidivism were analyzed as well as the word choices, emphasis, and the descriptions that were used in responses. The analysis of the language culture in correctional organizations suggests that the adaptation by staff members and inmates to the perspectives of the organization maintains the status quo and perpetuates the correctional organizational culture. Ricoeur (1991) posits that what is considered self-talk may instead be discourse through which individuals absorb themselves into the organization. The inmate who, through interaction with staff and other absorbed inmates, becomes assimilated is (1) less suited to developing skills unrelated to prison life and (2) less able to internalize a changed perspective toward self. The woman offender can, therefore, increase the likelihood of her return to prison by becoming co-opted by the system.

THE DATA

Three types of data are used in this study. One type is responses to open-ended questions from the staff and inmate surveys. Responses to the surveys were transcribed verbatim into manuscripts according to specific questions.

The second type of data was audiotaped interviews that were conducted with both staff and inmates. Six staff members were chosen from a convenience pool. The staff interviewees reflect the two major racial groups employed at Site 1 (African American and white) and both of the genders working in the organization. Six women inmates were also chosen from a convenience pool; these interviewees also reflect the racial representation at Site 1 (e.g., the inmates self-identified as African American, Native American, Chicano, and Caucasian). The interviews were conducted during May and December of 1991. The audiotaped interviews were conducted in privacy, with only the researcher and a staff member or an inmate present. Coffee or a soft drink was offered, but no incentives were given. The researcher and the interviewee sat facing each other alongside a long table in a conference room. The interviews began with pragmatic open-ended questions in order to allow the interviewee to become accustomed to the taping process. Open-ended questions and overview questions were used to prompt the participant to discuss topics relevant to the rising rate of incarcerated women and recidivism.

Using McCracken's (1988) concept of the "long interview," the interview provides a framework in which the subject can share perspectives, topics, and opinions that fixed surveys cannot anticipate. The researcher used questions such as these as a catalyst: "Tell me about your first day as an employee." "What was it like when you were incarcerated the first time?" "Why do you think so many women are returning to prison?" Both staff and inmates had much to say about correctional organizations and reasons for incarceration and recidivism. However, the inmates were more forthcoming in the interviews than on the surveys. Staff members, on the whole, were more formal and less open in the survey than in the interview. Some staff members became quite open during the face-to-face interview and shared insider information. The audiotaped interviews were transcribed verbatim into manuscripts. The researcher used both original and transcribed data for analyses.

The third type of data is observational descriptions of Site 1 in the form of field notes by the researcher. The analysis of the language culture of this women's prison includes all three data sets.

STAFF: PURPOSES OF CORRECTIONS AND REASONS FOR RECIDIVISM

While both the inmate and staff surveys were broad in the topics and abundant data were collected, this analysis addresses the staff members' opinions on the purposes of corrections and the reasons for recidivism.

The Survey

Responses to the following staff survey questions were analyzed:

Question #32:   What do you think the purpose of "corrections" is?

Question #73:   What is the major reason for women returning to prison after they have been released?

Staff responses to question #32 regarding the purpose of corrections can be categorized in several ways. One area consisted of repeating versions of the official mission statement of this state corrections organization: "To protect the public; to protect the employee; to protect the offender." Repetition of the mission statement, in varying forms, in the anonymous survey is a first clue to understanding the language culture of the staff. In the written responses, the formal language of the in-house and off-site training was very apparent. Employees who have contact with inmates go through a four-week, 40-hours-per-week training before beginning their employment. This training by the Oklahoma State Department of Corrections is at a location where the participants live, eat, and work together for a month (with the exception of weekends). Upon arrival at their new place of employment, many attend another three to five days of in-house training and orientation. Very little of this training is directly related to their new positions. Rather, the training focuses on the policies, rules, regulations, and values of the correctional agency. In their surveys, many employees repeated the perspectives of the organization.

While spelling and grammatical corrections have been made, the responses are the words of the staff members. Some of the responses that reflect the mission orientation are:

- To protect the public
- To protect employees
- To protect offenders
- To keep the felon in a safe (sanitary, positive, humane) place

These and other organizational rhetorical responses reinforce the avowed mission of the Department of Corrections.

Another category of answers about the purposes of corrections was related to the declared goal of all modern correctional centers—rehabilitation:

- To model good living standards
- To empower the employee
- To develop the offender
- To change offenders' concepts of their lives

- To set a good example
- To prevent recidivism
- To provide tools to offenders so that those who are willing can change their behavior and become contributing citizens

The concept of rehabilitation is also implicit in many of the other responses:

- To educate
- To make productive people ready to enter society
- To improve the quality of life for all society
- To give them [inmates] a chance for self-fulfillment
- To give opportunity

The answers listed above emphasize the contribution of corrections to the greater good of society, implying that such a contribution is an embedded value in this correctional organization. These values are both explicit and implicit during the initial training and the yearly required 40 hours of off-site training for "inmate contact" employees.

In addition to the mission statement variations and the "better society" responses, several staff gave replies that implicitly and explicitly say that the purpose of corrections is to punish, deter, or carry out mandates of the courts.

- To house convicted felons
- To keep [inmates] off the street
- To punish by locking up
- Separation of felons from society
- Discipline
- To [keep] from illegal or dangerous activity
- To confine
- To contain
- To deter people from bad habits
- For retribution
- To carry out sentences set by laws
- To follow orders of the court

Answers regarding the purposes of corrections are laden with perspectives of the organization as a culture, suggesting the nature of the relationships in the organization. In speaking about the rehabilitation of inmates, the respondents speak of themselves as "models of good behavior." They present the employee (self) as one of the beneficiaries of reformed inmates. That is, staff members responding in this manner believe that the successful accomplishment of the purpose of corrections (although they may not agree on what that purpose is) benefits themselves. Such success serves the needs of "corrections" and "employees" and "show[s] care and concern to the employees" and allows the employees to "correct by training, teaching, helping, [and] counseling." This altruistic view of the role of staff, by staff, was not reflected in staff oral interviews or inmate written or oral responses, suggesting that the formality of written responses is an important channel for the formal, bureaucratic language that controls the image of the organization.

Question #73 is: "What is the major reason for women returning to prison after they have been released?" The responses to this question can be categorized into two areas: (1) personal/internal reasons and (2) external reasons.

Repeatedly, staff responded that the personal/internal reasons for recidivism among women inmates were that they

- had no social skills
- were unable to be self-sufficient
- had not broken ties with old friends
- kept old habits
- did drugs
- didn't recognize consequences of actions
- couldn't provide for self (or family)
- lacked networking with recovering people
- took easy way out
- had no moral values
- found it easier on the "inside" than "on the street"
- refused to accept responsibilities
- were unable to adjust to a clean, lawful, and productive life
- enjoyed the thrill of committing crimes

These personal/internal reasons represent the traditional view of women offenders. The opposites of each of these reasons are elements of the profile of mainstream society, a society that is basically Anglo and middle-class. Staff members' descriptions of individuals who are in control of their lives would include the opposites of these attributes. The positive attributes are elements in the profiles of staff and those who work in the system.

The second category is that of external causation. This list is also one that is espoused by the training information and in-service education for corrections employees. The organizational perspective allows for the external reasons why women offenders recidivate. Some staff members respond with the following reasons:

- Society's attitude toward convicted felons
- No training, education, or life skills
- People who aren't willing to take a chance on felons
- No self-help groups or support systems or aftercare programs
- Lack of change in society
- No family bonding

This category is much smaller in length and scope. According to staff, the woman offender recidivates more often because of personal/internal reasons than because of external reasons. This perspective is an acceptable and collective correctional organizational concept.

The Audiotaped Interviews

Audiotaped interviews of the employees differed in part from the written responses in that more negative responses regarding inmates, the organization, and the mission of rehabilitation of inmates were spoken than written. The extended time with staff allowed for elaboration by staff members and gave them the opportunity to bring up subjects freely. The tapes ranged from 25 to 42 minutes in length.

One area of opinion expressed by all but one staff member who had worked with both women and men inmates was that men were "easier to work with. . . . They are more respectful; they are more accepting. . . . They know when you've done something for them, and they're more appreciative of that." The general consensus of staff members, however, was that women expected personal treatment and would continue to ask for personal attention. However, women inmates didn't always present themselves as grateful enough to justify the staff's extra effort for them, and the employees were unhappy about that lack of response. Male prisoners, in the opinion of these staff, "played the game" of good prisoner better than women. The male staff member who disagreed with this position suggested that although women were more petty and expressed themselves more about their individual situations, women in prison were less physically violent than men. He therefore preferred working with women over men prisoners at the maximum security prison where he had previously worked.

In the taped interviews, the staff were less divided in opinions regarding purposes of corrections and reasons for recidivism than in the written responses. Fewer employees discussed the stated mission of the corrections agency. In the interviews, more staff members stated that corrections should be about rehabilitation, but few were convinced that prisons for women offenders rehabilitate them. Rather, staff members were aware that, in general, programs are less available for women than for men prisoners. The staff agreed that (1) educational opportunities are not adequate for women, (2) job training slots are too few, (3) the substance abuse programs do not have enough slots for the prison population, and (4) the substance abuse programs are not as effective as desired.

Ironically, the same staff members then suggested that even if these deficiencies were addressed, the women offenders would recidivate because of personal/internal reasons such as the ones listed earlier from the written responses. The individual staff member is aware of problems in the organization; however, most employees adopt the organizational perspective that a woman offender is a product of her own choices. Societal problems may be a factor, but for the staff, who are members of the organizational culture, women recidivists return, ultimately, because of their own personal deficiencies.

A recurring theme among staff regarding the personal/internal reasons for recidivism was related to the fact that women in prison enjoy a life better than any they have had "on the street." Comparing the "good life" of the woman offender who is in prison to the terrible life of the same woman "on the street," staff noted that these women enjoyed (1) regular and, generally, well-balanced meals, (2) structure for their lives, (3) no responsibilities for their children, parents, lovers, husbands, and so forth, (4) dependable and predictable responses to their behaviors, (5) health care, and (6) relationships with other women that are often deeper than previous family ties. Indeed, this perception is one shared by many staff members and even some of the women inmates. Its implications, however, are not just the superficial concept that prison provides predictable care. This shared view by members of a correctional organization suggests at least tacit approval of women offenders who unconsciously or, in some cases, consciously choose to return to prison. The question raised by these perspectives is, What effect does the adoption of this organizational perspective by inmates and the adaptation of the inmates to prison have on recidivism?

INMATES: REASONS FOR INCARCERATION AND RECIDIVISM

Survey question #82 on the inmate survey is: "What do you feel contributed to your ongoing trouble with the law?"

The Survey

As with those of staff, inmates' responses may be divided into personal/internal and external categories. In addition, the various responses suggest the influence of substance abuse.

As Kelley (1972) suggests, few people give personal/internal reasons for negative behavior. In their responses, few women cited personal/internal reasons; those who did mentioned

- Just wanted to
- Power
- Escape from reality
- Low self-esteem
- Depression
- Excitement
- Boredom
- Wrong choice
- Ignorance

These respondents were characterized by few explanations or variety in answers. They did not answer many of the other open-ended questions. Their answers were sparse, with few adjectives or adverbs and little clarification. They justified neither their answers nor their actions, as others did in answers that suggested external reasons. The lack of self-explanation or revelation is consistent with the behavior of individuals with low self-esteem.

Women who said that their recidivist behaviors were externally caused gave the following responses:

- Money
- Battering
- Addiction
- Attorney
- Family problems
- Sexual abuse
- Prejudice
- Association with bad people
- Innocent
- No skills or job
- Police
- No Counseling
- Men (e.g., husband, boyfriend, father)
- Co-dependency
- No education
- Being away from family
- Being alone
- The system

These answers were expressive, expansive, and colorfully punctuated with both adjectives, adverbs, and elaborate punctuation. Sentences rather than one-word answers were used. The inmates justified their behavior, giving reasons based on their perception of the events.

The explanation of substance abuse as a cause of recidivism was woven through many answers. Contrary to the staff, the inmates perceived substance abuse as neither an internal nor an external reason. Rather, they discussed substance abuse as a separate problem, a problem that related to other reasons, both personal/internal and external. The use of this explanation was often a separate reason with little elaboration other than mentioning it in relationship to a personal/internal or external cause.

The Audiotaped Interviews

The audiotaped interviews of inmates were important to this study and ranged between 35 and 60 minutes in length. The opportunities for an inmate to talk about her life with a person who is neither staff nor another inmate is a rare opportunity for women offenders. As a result, all but one interviewee spoke with apparent openness, choosing to provide unguarded opinions about their daily lives, their perceptions about the correctional organization and its members, and their opinions about recidivism. Only one woman who was asked chose not to be interviewed, and only one of the interviewees appeared to be giving token responses. She was reserved in her manner and chose to limit the discussion to superficial topics.

The interviews with the inmates provided insights into the daily lives of women offenders and their views of corrections. One of the broad questions used in the interview addressed the process of entering a correctional institution both the first time and subsequent times. Inmate responses on the socialization process by the organization (both formal and informal) revealed the importance of bureaucratic language in maintaining the organization with its perceived purpose and preservation of resources.

Inmates, in similar fashion as the staff, defined the purposes of corrections in organizational terms that reflect the historic purposes of such institutions: (1) to isolate offenders from society and (2) to rehabilitate offenders. However, they said that everyone is human and everyone makes mistakes, presenting this generalization about inmate conduct (in several versions) as an implicit acceptance about the need for isolation. The differences in inmate and staff talk were subtle, in that the explicit explanations about the purposes of corrections were indirectly given by inmates as they talked about the court system, their entry and reentry into prison, and their daily lives.

Significant to this study is the circuitous manner of responses of the inmates to discussions dealing with the system. They began with examples and exceptions to regular activity. They clarified or discussed the crux of a situation after these examples, and they then returned to the main topic or let the examples lead to new topics. This type of talk reflects the skills necessary to the "good" inmate. That is, the inmate who has adapted to prison adopts the language of bureaucracy, in which indirect speech, formal channels, and the circumvention of paths of authority must be developed in order to accomplish personal goals and to function successfully within the organization's culture.

In most of the interviews, the questions regarding first entry and recurring entries into the system revealed the following aspects of corrections. The entry to any correctional center begins with a move from a county or local jail to a state central processing prison. Isolation from other inmates, family, and friends; medical evaluation; evaluation of inmates for assignment to a minimum, medium, or maximum security institution; and deliberate limitation of information about both the process and future

activities characterize this state of incarceration. The purpose of such a
process has long been established in the military model of orientation to
enhance the dependency of the clients on the organizational system. An
inmate noted:

I went to Smithville [all names are changed for purposes of confidentiality] and
I stayed there two weeks. . . . I got there and . . . I couldn't believe it. . . . I was
stunned because . . . my incarceration at Jamestown . . . was more open, you
know, than it was there, and then it was like a shock treatment for me because
you couldn't come out of your rooms. . . . In Smithville you're locked down most
of the day, get to come out for meals, and in the evenings they'll let you out for
like a couple of hours.

Several of the women discussing Smithville Processing Center talked
about the differences in their experiences when, at different times in the
process, they were placed in one-person cells or, during times of overcrowding, they were placed two or three persons to a cell. Attempts by the
inmates to obtain information during the first incarceration at this processing center usually resulted in no information or rebuffs by officials. The
processing was a formalized procedure designed to (1) obtain official
information about inmates, (2) make the inmate dependent on the system,
and (3) limit information available to inmates. Significant to the various
recitals of this experience was the information that recidivating offenders
did not attempt to obtain information during their second and succeeding
processing experiences.

Further, they watched as newcomers tried to get individual assistance
or information, but the previous offenders often did not attempt to tell the
newcomers about the futility of such requests. Most recidivists believed
that the firsthand experience of the refusal was a necessary experience for
the new inmate.

The decision to let newcomers learn in their own way is not a unilateral
decision for inmates. While inmates have differing perceptions about the
need for adaptation to the system, different behaviors control the inmates'
decision to informally socialize others. A long-term inmate in her fifties
who was a recidivist talked about her change from a person who sought
out newcomers in order to help them adjust to the system to a person who
minded her own business and reserved her energies for surviving her time
in the organization.

The organizational perspective of a correctional institution is that
inmates should be as uninvolved with other inmates as possible. The
organization restricts activity such as (1) loaning toiletries, (2) assisting

another inmate in personal ways (e.g., taking another's duties, doing another's personal chores, etc.), and (3) sharing possessions (e.g., clothes, radios, etc.). That is, many of the normal type of friendship activities exercised by most women on the outside are either actively discouraged or strictly forbidden by the rules of the organization. Some inmates seek to circumvent these restrictions and to network and make coalitions with other inmates. Others begin their incarceration by strictly adhering to the rules. Yet others choose to help newcomers at first, but later choose to adopt the organizational perspective of proper behavior in the belief that they are better off.

Inmates' formal socialization into the system consists of two to three days of orientation. The reality is that some inmates never go through the orientation process because of overcrowding or interruptions in scheduling. Some inmates said that the formal orientation was not valuable because it was too vague, so they had not missed anything. Others said they made friends with other inmates because they had to ask questions. Still others said that other inmates gave them faulty information, either through ignorance or through deliberate attempts to hurt the newcomer.

Throughout these discussions, the women referred to the purposes of corrections, often through negative accounts of experiences. Several women began the discussion with, "If they want me to stay straight, then why don't they . . . " The "why don't they" included suggestions such as the following: (1) provide job training that is useful for all types of people, (2) have education available for everyone who wants it, (3) have a variety of self-help programs, (4) have more effective substance abuse therapeutic programs, and (5) have as many opportunities for women as they do for men. The implication is that the correctional organization is there to rehabilitate them. They most often asked why more substance abuse programs were not available and why those that were in place were not working.

The women also discussed "how to do time" and what they thought about being in prison. One woman said, "People say that you're institutionalized because you settle back and you just do your time and don't let your time do you. . . . My first few incarcerations [were] like that." Another woman also talked about adapting to prison.

I was, can't believe I'm gonna go to prison. So when I got to prison, I was kind of surprised because you can't tell a murderer from a bogus check writer here. . . . They're all people, and now that I'm like one of them I don't look at what they've done and decide [to] judge 'em. . . . You just look at who they are now. . . . in fact, my best friends that I've made have all been murderers, and I told my mom I don't know why that is but everyone who I've made real close friends with has been murderers. . . . you know, they think I'm brainwashed or something, but you just got to bear with it.

Regarding recidivism, one inmate said:

First off, I have to tell you there's . . . some advantages for some people; [that's] why they keep coming back. One, you know . . . they were locked up for so long, they were used to this system, [and] when they walk out there, it's a whole different world. They don't know nobody, but they try, you know, they have the ability to try, but most of them fail. . . . Some say because it's hard out there. . . . They couldn't communicate with nobody; they couldn't get themselves together; it was like they were helpless out there, and the only thing they know how to do was get themselves in here and do what they were used to. So it was kinda like a revolving door for them.

A woman who was a recidivist believed that she could tell who would return to prison.

I can tell you who's gonna show back up. . . . They don't have any ambition; they don't have goals or any dreams. They just want out. I mean we all want out. . . . I think a lot of people just come to accept it. . . . I think it's because they can come here and lay around and kick back and let somebody else take care of their kids, that's what I think it is. Stop and think about it.

The same woman says that the way that she could tell who would not return is

a lot of them that aren't coming back are ones that are completely leaving their environment. . . . The reason, I think, . . . is 'cause they've made a decision. Some time in their lives, whether it was here or in jail or wherever they were, [they decided that] they're not gonna come back. But they gotta go with that decision.

Regarding the effects of incarceration, one inmate said:

You're indoctrinated from the time you leave Smithville . . . . how you're put into a cell, the steel door, you cannot talk to your family, there's no mail correspondence for awhile. . . . I didn't even question, it never occurred to me to say that I'd like to—it just didn't. If they said to do this, I said, "OK" because I know at that point I'd lost control of any decisions. So, you just flow with it. Once you get into the system, it's real hard to get out of the system. . . . It doesn't matter what you've accomplished in here.

This woman went on to discuss the despair that long-term residents feel when they have taken all of the classes that they can, worked in all of the areas, and have used all of the meager facilities available to them. They perceive that growth is not possible on a personal or organizational basis.

Several inmates in the interviews addressed the issue of why more women per capita are incarcerated in Oklahoma than in other states. Their responses are related to the socioeconomic and political climate in Oklahoma, summarized as follows:

1. Oklahoma is "backward" economically. Therefore, women are in financial trouble; they get in trouble because of economic needs.
2. Judges in Oklahoma think that women should be better than men; when women do the same crimes as men, they get "time" instead of "walking" on probation.
3. Oklahoma is a Bible belt state, so judges and courts are stricter about crimes; other states wouldn't give "hard time" for the same crime.

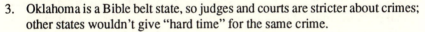

Some of the staff members, ironically, suggested these same reasons for the high rates of both incarceration and recidivism. The words of the inmates summarize the inmates' responses to the issues of both incarceration and recidivism.

CONCLUSIONS

The responses of both employees and inmates regarding purposes of corrections and reasons for recidivism provide insights into the ongoing problems of the high rates of incarceration and recidivism for women offenders. Additionally, revelation of the co-optation of organizational perspectives by both employees and inmates is important to the understanding of the roles of both staff members and inmates to the perpetuation of correctional organizations.

One site of conflict that reveals a major dilemma between the inmate and the organization is the correctional organization's perception that confinement and rehabilitation are aggregate, as contrasted with the inmates' belief that confinement and rehabilitation are personal. The organization believes that it must protect its resources and maintain the status quo. Providing personal rather than aggregate confinement and rehabilitation would endanger both the resources and the status quo. The co-optation of employees and inmates provides the organization's defense against depletion of resources and change.

The revelations of the inmates regarding recidivism reveals their perspectives that the skills necessary to be a "good" inmate are not necessarily the same skills that are needed to remain on the outside. Attitudes about why some women inmates return are rooted in views that the correctional organization makes people adapt to its culture and that this adaptation— the co-opting of the inmate to the system—results in the return of many inmates to the organization. The organizational structure, rules, and perspectives of the roles of the inmates and employees may in fact discourage the development of the life skills and attitudes that could enable an inmate to avoid recidivism.

The question remains: Does the co-opted inmate become less successful in developing skills unrelated to prison life, and is she less able to internalize a changed perspective toward self, thereby increasing the likelihood of her return to prison? The findings of this study suggest that this is the case. However, more study of the language culture of correctional organizations should be undertaken. With greater understanding of the relationship between language culture and recidivism among women offenders, organizational changes and programs for women offender education can be proposed with greater confidence.

11 Toward an Integrated Theory of Female Criminality and Incarceration

Garry L. Rolison

As Leonard (1982) develops, criminological theory has paid scant attention to women offenders. This chapter fashions a theoretical frame for understanding women's experiences with crime and incarceration through the prisms of feminism and critical theory. This provisional theoretical frame is supplemented with more traditional perspectives in criminology. In particular, the chapter draws upon the insights of labeling theory, differential association, and subcultural theory to round out the perspective. However, patriarchy is theoretically privileged in the work's attempt to classify, order, and categorize women's criminological experiences.

FEMALE CRIME AND RISK OF INCARCERATION

In the past 15 years, there has been a great deal of research flurry with respect to the putative rise in female criminality. Much of that research has grown out of reaction to the work of Freda Adler (1975). In particular, Adler argues that the rise in female criminality has been the result of increased assertiveness of women occasioned by the women's movement. Simon (1975) takes a more sober view, accepting that the women's movement has fundamentally changed the social circumstances of women but explaining the rise in female criminality as the result of newly increased economic opportunity for women to commit crime.

Gora (1982) questions both Adler and Simon and presents longitudinal data that dispute the putative relationship between the women's movement and increased female criminality. Following Hoffman-Bustamante (1973) and Harris (1977), Gora offers a revision of traditional criminological theory to explain the differential rates of criminality between women and men. Her conclusion is that once class-specific sex role socialization experiences are explored, traditional criminological perspectives can explain much about female criminality. Hence, despite her critiques of Adler and Simon, Gora concludes that changes in sex role socialization alter women's propensity to commit crime. In short, Gora doesn't travel very far from the thesis that the women's movement may have had much to do with the rise in female criminality. In contrast to Adler's, Simon's, and Gora's postulations, this chapter puts forth a theory of women's criminality that has patriarchy at its center.

THE CENTRALITY OF PATRIARCHY

Following Walby (1990) *patriarchy* is defined "as a system of social structures and practices in which men dominate, oppress and exploit women" (p. 20). However, the category of "women" is not a composite construction. In particular, it is recognized that important distinctions exist among women and that different women are oppressed differently. Immediately class, race, sexual orientation, and sexual behavior come to mind as different nodes around which different women are further oppressed within a general system of patriarchy. Additionally, other less explored nodes of oppression present themselves, including age, weight, color, physical impediment, height, and other socially constructed physical markers of difference from the patriarchal norm of the feminine aesthetic (Bartky, 1992). Nevertheless, again following Walby (1990, p. 16), it is possible to talk of a structure of patriarchy that extends past and through these different nodes of oppression despite their variations among different women. Indeed, within the context of patriarchal oppression, it is posited that these factors are mutually constitutive of patriarchy itself and as such offer a template of social knowledge about women that can be and is used to construct individual women into what Foucault (1977) might term "objects of discipline."

In general, it is expected that women who are black, from poor families, perceived as nonheterosexual or hyperheterosexual, considered to be heterosexually unappealing (e.g., middle-aged, overweight, of dark complexion), unfeminine (e.g., strong willed, coarse, and emotional), or as having devalued feminine traits (e.g., gossipy, talkative, and irrational) will be the most typical female objects of discipline (Bartky, 1992). It is further posited that these characteristics are compounded by a legal system that continues to define most criminal behavior as a male province (Worrall, 1990). The next section discusses how in combination these factors facilitate the making of women involved in criminal behavior potential objects of discipline by both private and public patriarchy. (For a discussion of the differences and the relationship between private and public patriarchy, see Walby [1990]).

Constructing Female Objects of Discipline

In beginning this section, it is probably helpful to start with a heuristic example of how patriarchy predisposes certain women to become objects of discipline. Consider the ordinary realities of living in a poor neighborhood. In such communities there is a greater likelihood of contact with police and hence a greater probability of arrest. After arrest there is less likelihood of affording a private lawyer and therefore greater likelihood of incarceration. These events are to some extent occasioned simply by structural inequality. The important point, however, is that criminality is construed not only for those arrested but for the community itself. In essence, the community becomes, in public perception, a "bad" place—a crime-ridden community. Partially as a result of this representation, agents of social control are empowered to act in these communities in ways that produce and reproduce this perception. In particular, the practice of constantly surveilling and questioning residents perpetuates the perception of a "bad place." This then becomes the context through which further surveillance is made possible. In essence, simply living in these communities places individuals at increased risk of arrest through increased surveillance.

As Foucault (1977) points out, surveillance is the cornerstone of disciplinary power. Surveillance gives to agents of social control the ability to develop a file on individuals and later punish those individuals for specific transgressions. In other words, given that the commission of crime is dispersed throughout all groups, the intense surveillance of some groups allows agents of social control the capability of exercising discipline over those individuals. This capability is further enhanced by the ability of social agents to construct files on individuals that in turn allow the transfer of these transgressions across different institutions of social control. For example, files that are routinely manufactured at the welfare department and the housing authority on women who have become dependent upon public patriarchy hold the potential for generating subpoenas in criminal cases and even have the capability of generating criminal complaint. As poverty and gender converge and poor women come increasingly under the purview of public patriarchy as occasioned by conservative shifts in the welfare state (e.g., increased record keeping on public welfare recipients and public housing residents), the incarceration of women should increase partially because of the proliferation of surveillance and file keeping. It is postulated that this will especially be the case for those women who, because of class and race, come to be concentrated in identifiable communities where surveillance by social control agents is normative.

File creation is central in another aspect in that it creates the capability to allow the transfer of transgressions across not only different institutions of social control, but across almost every social situation and interaction. In short, the keeping of records for these women has the potential to create what Goffman (1963) has called a spoiled identity. More to the point, persons on whom records are kept are always open to the possibility of being discredited privately as well as surveilled by the state. That is, these women can be negatively labeled by both intimates and strangers.

There is a close link between private and public patriarchy, surveillance, and women as objects of discipline. Simply put, women who have male associates that come to the attention of the state are likely to have their name, address, and identity also known by the state. As a result, their activities are likely to be publicly scrutinized and their association with such men taken to be evidence of deviance. However, the relationship here is complexly intertwined with contradictions between public and private patriarchy. For instance, some aspects of private patriarchy (e.g., woman as male helpmate and confidante) tend to predispose women to become involved in the criminal activities of their surveilled partners. Since aiding and abetting in the criminal activities of others is considered a crime, women who operate within these norms of private patriarchy become criminal simply through their association with criminal men. In short, a woman who associates with "bad" men in relations of private patriarchy becomes in the gaze of public patriarchy a *bad* woman.

The dilemma between private and public patriarchy has a racial and class component inasmuch as it is often poor men from oppressed racial groups who, according to Merton (1957), become *innovators* in their pursuit of wealth and power, that is, who become criminal. To the degree that cross-gender relationships are still relatively class and racially homogeneous, then women involved with these men on the one hand become objects of discipline by public patriarchy due to their involvement with bad men, and on the other hand become objects of discipline by these men because they are seen as bad or devalued women. Given this mix, abuse of these women by the men in their lives and lack of intervention by agents of social control can be expected. In short, it is postulated that these women learn early that they are devalued not only by their boyfriends and spouses but by society and public patriarchy because they are involved with bad men. It is posited that these women are likely to have low self-esteem, feel low mastery over the world, and distrust authority. In short, they display feelings of alienation and seek to escape those feelings through a host of coping strategies, most typically through drugs and alcohol and more generally through a craving for excitement and fun. The resultant life-style then becomes part of the way that these women reinforce both the construction of themselves as bad women and their continued association with bad men.

Chesney-Lind's (1978) work on female juvenile delinquents has developed a similar line of argument around female criminality. However, Chesney-Lind starts with the family (i.e., the father) at its core. Specifically, she begins with the empirical finding that many women offenders were the victims of violence and sexual abuse at home. She notes that since these women as girls lacked credibility with agents of social control, they were able to escape domestic abuse only by running away, and they learned to survive through criminal means and their sexuality. The exploitation of their sexuality then served to label these young women as "bad" women. They in turn are treated as such by the men they are with, who continue to abuse them as adults. As these women strike out against their abuse and abusers, they are incarcerated.

The perspective employed here deemphasizes the life-event sequence that starts with the home and instead emphasizes the interaction of women with bad men at other points during the life course. That is, it may matter more that these women are involved with bad men than it does that they experienced an earlier pattern of violence, sexual abuse, and runaway behavior that leads to that involvement. Certainly violence, sexual abuse, and runaway behavior contribute to the process of how women get involved with bad men, as Chesney-Lind develops. It is suggested here that public and private patriarchy interact to doubly label these women as "bad" and that it is this interaction that gives much of the character to women's crimes. Indeed, this perspective accounts for a greater range of women's crimes than Chesney-Lind's perspective, in that it indicates how women operating in the context of private patriarchy come to assist men in the commission of crime. That is, the supportive dimension of nurturance and helping behavior they provide for criminal men often accounts for the putative criminality of women. This perspective also explains women's crimes of violence against their direct abusers and crimes committed for economic and addictive support.

To sum up, it is expected that devalued women have few options against abuse in either the private or the public sphere. That is, the state will not intercede in matters of domestic abuse, and boyfriends, lovers, or husbands will not intercede in matters of arrest and incarceration. Finally, it is posited that women involved with bad men are at risk of incarceration not simply because they strike out at their abusers but also because they participate, sometimes through coercion, sometimes through nurturance and support, in the crimes committed by criminal men.

Misplaced Chivalry: Explaining the Incarceration of Women

Private and public patriarchy are intertwined also in the incarceration of women. Since private patriarchy considers women's role of mother as primary (Chodorow, 1978), it is the assumption of most men that this role is paramount with respect to considerations of incarceration. In other words, men assume that women may commit crime but won't do time because of the patriarchy's respect for motherhood. While, Simon (1975) has found some empirical evidence to suggest that judges are likely to consider motherhood in sentencing, probably more instructive are her findings that this does not extend to arrest and probation. In essence, the assumption of motherhood as a buffer against female incarceration is likely to be overestimated. This is because of fundamental conflicting perceptions about mothering between private and public patriarchy.

The view of private patriarchy that motherhood is a buffer against incarceration ignores public patriarchy's desire to label and punish women who transgress acceptable norms of femininity. More fundamentally, it ignores that motherhood from the point of view of public patriarchy is less a job and more a responsibility of socialization. Therefore, a "bad" woman is a woman for whom the motherhood function is to be removed. If anything, incarceration of "bad" women accomplishes this task well.

This process, however, is contingent on a number of factors. That is, the establishment of a bad reputation is, in accord with the precepts of labeling theory, a negotiated identity (Becker, 1963). Evidence of the identity must to some extent be realized and accepted both by the labeled woman and the labeler. That is, the woman must acknowledge some pattern of unwillingness to socialize her children or future children to middle-class norms. To the degree that the woman is not a violent offender against the family, then evidence that shows her to be a "good mother" or "good partner" will serve to mitigate incarceration. Simon finds evidence of this in her studies on sentencing. If on the other hand, she shows acceptance of alternative norms for her children, she is likely to be punished.

Here we have an interesting area of congruence between labeling theory and the differential association perspective of criminal behavior. In essence, women who participate in a subculture that accepts criminal activity as normative place themselves at risk of being labeled bad women, accepting that label, and opening themselves to risk of incarceration independent of the impact of surveillance and file keeping mentioned previously. To the eyes of public patriarchy, acceptance of criminal behavior either through participation in criminal activity or association with criminal men is prima facie evidence of being an unfit mother.

The stress on mothering is even more encompassing than indicated here. Again, drawing on Merton (1957) we can postulate that the defining role of women can lead them to either innovate or escape their mother status. In particular, many women who are single parents can be expected to engage in monetary crimes to support their children. This results from two sources: (1) private and public patriarchy that still allow men to escape the responsibilities of financially caring for children and (2) a capitalist society that does not provide adequate income for the jobs of women or the employment of racially oppressed and class-oppressed women and men. These factors go a long way in explaining escapism by women from the pressures of mothering. Given these factors, high rates of substance abuse, reported incidences of child neglect, and increases in female criminal behavior among poor single mothers can be expected.

The process just described is impacted by racial oppression. It is to be remembered that African Americans are the most communally segregated group in the United States and that nearly one out of two black families with children are female headed. Moreover, the majority of these families are poor and likely to be concentrated in urban ghettos. Consequently, poor African American women are more easily surveilled, and these women are the ones most likely to find themselves in the system of public patriarchy; as a result, they come to be defined as "bad" women. Given this sequence of events, it is expected that poor black women are more commonly labeled as "bad" women and incarcerated. The next section takes up this discussion more directly by concentrating focus on the prison as a site where the inculcation of these values can occur through processes of oppression, negotiation, and resistance between inmates and staff.

WOMEN'S PRISONS: SITES OF REPRESSION

In 1893, Durkheim (1933) indicated that law and punishment serves two purposes in society, restitution and repression. In this section, concern is with the latter and its primary site in modern society, the prison.

The defining characteristic of repressive law and, therefore, prisons is the punishment of individuals who break core norms, beliefs, and values.

Given that criminal behavior for the most part is still perceived to be a male province, women who break the law suffer the double impact of not only violating a given social norm, but violating their sex role expectations as well (Worrall, 1990, p. 31). To a large extent this double violation helps to determine the character of women's prisons.

Though crucial as a beginning point to understand law and punishment in modern society, the Durkheimian view of repressive law fails to acknowledge that members of different cultural groups may not share the norms of the dominant group and that this serves not only as a source of potential conflict, but of oppression as well. In short, the view unwittingly posits cultural consensus where there may be none and ignores the reality that dominant cultural groups often have the power, acted upon or not, to define cultural difference itself as criminality. (Stuart Hall and colleagues [1978] have made a similar point about the relationship between race and class.)

Prisons are places in which culturally different peoples often find themselves, and prisons come to reflect these differences in their very composition. Therefore, to understand prisons is to grasp at a very basic level that cultural conflict (i.e., conflict over norms, beliefs, and values) is an integral part of the reproduction of prison life. Much of this has to do with the special nature of prisons themselves. Prisons are structures in which power is manifestly practiced unidirectionally. That is, staff exercise absolute power over inmates. Orders are given and the expectation is that they will be obeyed. However, as Weber (1968) points out, power for commanding and obeying based upon a common, agreed-upon norm, is multidimensional and hierarchical. Indeed, it is fruitful to view power as ranging on a continuum from force to authority. Force refers to the application of threat of physical coercion, whereas authority is legitimated power. However, in prison, show of force always lurks in the background because the object in question is the behavior of the inmate. Ironically, given that the application of force is an inefficient use of power entailing high psychic and material cost, the tendency is for agents of social control and the objects of that control to attempt to transform force into authority. In order for this to happen, inmates must come to believe that what staff wants them to do is in their best interest—in essence, to accept that staff control over inmate behavior as in the inmate's best interest.

Staff are aware that inmates have the power to disrupt routine at any given moment, hence calling upon them to enact the inefficient use of force. The enaction of force by the staff is problematic as it entails making their exercise of power costly. Staff, therefore, seek to engage inmates in negotiation concerning reasons that rules are important at the level of values as well as, more specifically, in promoting the inmates' best interest. Additionally, negotiation occurs between staff and inmates as to the limits of each rule and its application. Hence, the two groups come to share a common perception about which rules are to be followed to the letter and which are minor and can be safely ignored. This process of negotiation forms the basis by which inmates can make individual determinations about staff and categorize them as "good" or "bad." This categorization in turn sets the mode by which the individual staff are reacted to in terms of the force/authority dimension. "Good staff" are likely to be able to request adherence to routine rules at times when "bad staff" are likely to encounter open resistance. In short, similar to the dynamics in Genovese's (1976) discussion of paternalism with respect to slavery, inmates are able to fashion their power over the observance of rules by judiciously testing the limits of rules and categorizing staff as "good" or "bad."

This negotiation of power between inmates and staff points to the contested nature of power, a basic point of Foucault (1977). For Foucault power works through the active resistance of those against which it is being exercised. This active resistance in turn sets the limits, contours, and basic nature of the power relationship as it is activated. As such, power is always contingent upon the actors involved. We may supplement this view of power by recognizing, along with Giddens (1979), that rules are congealed forms of power that are drawn upon in its construction. Hence, rules then become indicative both of power relations and the contests over power. By conceptualizing power as contested and oppression as physical coercion, the importance of establishing a common value orientation that is partially negotiated by inmates and staff becomes paramount.

Jensen (1991), in researching the same population that is used in this study, offers some insight into how this process occurs. She develops three social types of prisoners: convict, inmate, and resident. These types are represented in the argot used by prisoners at the facility and refer to both an *inmate code* and the pattern of interaction with staff by each of the types. The inmate code is focused around "not snitching" and "keeping to oneself." Both *convicts* and *residents* accept this code and keep to themselves about most issues. Inmates, however, are less likely to do so. With respect to staff interactions, the defining characteristics are frequency and type of interaction. In particular, convicts do not interact with staff unless it is absolutely necessary, and their pattern of interaction is not to complain. Residents, who in Jensen's (1991) study comprised 70 percent of her sample, interact with staff on a consistent basis but do not typically complain. Inmates are clearly antistaff in their sentiments but interact with staff frequently, especially to complain about the institution and other prisoners. Although Jensen's (1991) work appears to take these categories as fixed, there is good reason to suspect fluidity between them. Indeed, her research shows the groups to differ by age, times of incarceration, and other factors that indicate that different prisoners move into and out of these types. In short, interaction between and among prisoners and staff has much to do ·with the way in which these identities come to be constructed and reproduced.

Patriarchy and Prison Control

Women's prisons tend to be impacted not only by the general process of negotiation and development of authority relations just described, but also by patriarchy. Given that many of the staff members of prisons are male, they tend to bring patriarchal conceptions of womanhood to the prison environment. Moreover, these perceptions are often further impacted by class. That impact, paradoxically, stems from the fact that most prison COs (guards) and staff are drawn from the same social classes from which inmates come, the working and lower-middle classes. These classes are those segments in society in which class culture is heavily skewed toward private patriarchal expression as to the "proper" role of women. Added to this is a racial component that typically finds white males as either direct (e.g., COs) or indirect (e.g., wardens) authority figures over a population composed mostly of women of color. These factors point to the possibility of differential access to programs of vocational and moral education by women of color and white inmates. If, as is the case in dominant society, white men reserve femininity solely for white women, it can be expected that white women will receive greater guidance and emphasis on femininity (e.g., information on how to dress for job interviews) than will be the case for women of color. However, it may also be the case that white women who remain nonconformist to feminine ways will be treated as harshly if not more harshly than women of color.

These constructions by race and gender also have import regarding how power is negotiated. It can be expected that women of color will experience more attempts of direct force by staff as well as increased devaluation. These are the women who, being "unfeminine," are likely to be labeled troublemakers and accept that role. As a result, they are less likely to be involved in the negotiation of power relations and more likely to suffer the direct application of force and coercion (i.e., oppression). Therefore, these women can be expected to suffer more turndowns for privileges and freedom than their white counterparts, with the exception of those whites who do not conform to staff rules.

Work on prison life has focused on two major perspectives or models. These models are typically referred to as the *deprivation* and *importation* models. The first has the longer history in criminological theory and can be ultimately traced to Clemmer's (1958) work in the early forties entitled *The Prison Community* and his concept of prisonization, that is, the way in which inmates come to adapt to prison life. However, it was McCorkle and Korn's (1954) influential article on the resocialization of prisoners that was to give shape to the deprivation perspective. The article is important to us for two reasons. First, it clearly posits a process by which inmates come to reconfigure their social worlds in prison. Second, and more important, the article suggests that the greater degree to which inmates become prisonized, the greater will be their chances of recidivating. As such, the deprivation model is important to this work for both its content and its prediction.

The importation perspective has a much shorter history in criminological theory. Its beginning can be traced to John Irwin's pathbreaking book, *The Felon,* published in 1970. In addition to its substance, the perspective is of interest in that it was developed in conscious opposition to the deprivation perspective discussed earlier. The substance of the critique is the questioning of whether differences noted in prison subcultures are the result of adaptation to what Sykes (1958) has called the "pains of imprisonment" or to the subcultural differences brought by inmates to the prison. In short, is it the structures of prisons that develop particular modes of interaction among inmates, or is it the cultures that inmates bring to prison that do so?

Studies on women within prisons have tended to apply the importation perspective. The reason for this is straightforward. As Goodstein and Wright (1989, p. 236) point out, the importation model has as its main tenet that prison subculture reflects the inmate's preprison social world. This implies that different preprison experiences shape and mold the prison experience. As a result, different groups should be expected to have differing prison experiences and orientations to prison life based upon their orientation and experience. Since women's socialization experiences are different from men's, given the importation model, we should expect their adjustment to prison life to be different. Research has to a large extent borne this out. In particular, Ward and Kassebaum (1965) and Fox (1982), find that women in prison develop strong friendship bonds and create pseudofamilial relationships while incarcerated. This is very different from the prison life of men, in which traits of "toughness" and individual survival are most important. Indeed, one consistent finding in this area is that the nature of same-sex relationships differs substantially between male and female inmates. Whereas for men such relationships tend to be exploitative, for women these relationships tend to reflect emotional commitment (see Giallombardo, 1966). In short, it is apparent that women bring with them to prisons many of the expectations associated with their sex-role socialization to prison life.

In sum, it is expected that class, race, and sex-role socialization, along with staff preconceptions of each, will determine the ways in which different women express their prison experience as well as set the contours of that expression. Moreover, it is posited that these expressions are constituted anew during each interaction by inmate and staff, although the basic boundaries remain fixed and anchored by institutional rules.

SUMMARY

This chapter has attempted to build on the work of Chesney-Lind (1978) and Bartky (1992) in its explanation of female criminal behavior, while fundamentally relying on the distinction that Walby (1990) draws between public and private patriarchy as a structuring thread.

From Bartky's (1992) work, and following Foucault (1977), this chapter emphasizes the process of surveillance as a principle in the construction of women as objects of discipline. This approach allows an escape from any patriarchal essentialism (i.e., the notion that all women are oppressed equally) while maintaining an integrated perspective on women's crime with an open patriarchy at its core (i.e., women are made objects of discipline by and through patriarchy; however, these expressions differ according to women's race, class, and physical appearance). Bartky's (1992) work is supplemented by positing that acts of surveillance and discipline happen at both the community and the microscopic level. Hence, this work attempts to explain why some women are more likely to be arrested and incarcerated than others.

With respect to prison life, the chapter discusses power as a constitutive element in the construction of women's prison subculture. Drawing upon the work of Irwin (1970), the importation model is explored in an attempt to highlight the difference between female and male prison culture. Additionally, the importance of class-specific sex-role socialization is briefly discussed.

12   Conclusions

Beverly R. Fletcher and Dreama G. Moon

We began this book by looking at several reasons for undertaking a study of women prisoners: (1) the female prison population is growing at a significantly faster rate than the male prison population, (2) little research has been done on recidivism of female inmates, (3) women make up a larger percentage of the prison population in Oklahoma than they do nationwide, making Oklahoma an important place in which to study women inmates. Perhaps the most important reason for writing this book is that the results from our initial analyses have given insights into some of the problems of recidivating women prisoners, and we believe that this will have implications for both criminal justice practitioners and criminology theorists.

Recidivism, as used in the context of this book, is defined as the return of former inmates to prison resulting from committing a new crime or violating a probationary rule. Although this measure of recidivism is admittedly conservative, we chose it over other definitions because our main focus is on women's prison experiences. Also, we believe that defining recidivism as the return to prison is a practical and clear-cut way to measure recidivism.

Thus far, incarcerated women have received little help from prison reforms. Their facilities are inadequate and remote, opportunities for education and rehabilitation are few, and health care is poor. In women's prisons tranquilizers and drugs are used more often for social control than in men's prisons, and parental rights are more often taken away.

Women imprisoned in Oklahoma share many of the same life struggles and characteristics as women imprisoned throughout the country. Among those common experiences are abuses inflicted on them as children and/or adults, economic pressures, and substance addictions. This study, although conducted in the state of Oklahoma, provides insights that are useful throughout the country. In particular, we have drawn some conclusions about the impact of self-esteem on female recidivism, the importance of internal locus of control for preventing recidivism, the importance of education and practical ways to utilize that education, the need for support systems, the relationship of drug use to female recidivism, the likelihood of a history of abuse affecting recidivism, significant ethnic differences among women inmates that need to be considered when developing programs to combat recidivism, the death penalty as applied to female violent offenders, prison organizations and perspectives that may be useful for enhancing their effectiveness, correctional staff attitudes and their impact on female recidivism, the impact on recidivism of co-optation into prison culture, and the theoretical effect of public and private patriarchy on women's likelihood of becoming criminal. This information can serve to enhance the development of programs aimed at reducing recidivism among female prisoners everywhere.

SUMMARY OF RESULTS

Self Esteem

Results from this study indicate individual characteristics that are significantly related to higher levels of self-esteem: good health, internal locus of control, and social support. Promoting high levels of self-esteem in women is necessary if we are to intervene in the cycle of recidivism. These findings warrant a reevaluation of institutional programs and encourage the promotion of programs and policies that promote a sense of internality regarding locus of control and allow for the practical application of inmate education.

Substance Use

Rising incarceration rates for women are not divorced from the rising illegal use of prescription and nonprescription drugs in American society. National and state studies as well as the Project for Recidivism Research and Female Inmate Training data indicate that high percentages of women were either convicted for drug-related crimes or were under the influence of drugs or alcohol at the time of their current offense. While drug addiction has been well documented among males, less research has been devoted to the study of women and drugs. The scant literature and data from our study identify several trends regarding imprisoned women's drug abuse patterns and suggest alternative treatment techniques for women's addictions.

Abuse

Inmates who are abused are more likely to perceive themselves as having a problem with drugs or alcohol. Inmates who report being abused before the age of 18 are less likely to have a high school diploma than those who have not been abused and are more likely to encounter economic hardship as a result. The lives of female victims of abuse are profoundly affected by that abuse, and treatment is necessary if abused former offenders are to be averted from returning to prison.

African American Women in Prison

Data from this study highlight the disproportionate numbers of African American women in our nation's prisons. Significant differences between imprisoned African American women and other women inmates were found in five general areas: (1) family structure, (2) age at first arrest, (3) drug use pattern before incarceration, (4) incidence of physical and emotional abuse, and (5) levels of self-esteem. Although most intervention programs would be equally beneficial for all women in prison, these findings sensitize the reader to the group differences that call for the development of targeted programs for maximum effectiveness and relevancy to the woman inmate.

Death Row

The death penalty has been imposed on women since our nation's beginnings. The effect of regionalism, racism, and classism on the likelihood of a violent offender's receiving the death penalty have already been examined and studied by many who research capital punishment. There is a need for studies of death sentencing practices as they relate to women. It appears that women are sentenced more harshly than men for capital offenses. We need to take a closer look at why women are committing capital crimes. More information is needed about the conditions under which women are held on death row, and studies on the many variables that affect the sentencing of women to death are necessary.

Correctional Organizations

Organizations have been studied from many perspectives. This study examines how prisons differ from other types of organizations; we look at the characteristics prisons share with other types of organizations, the aspects of organizational communication that impact staff and inmates, the usefulness of organization development theory in addressing the problems of prison organizations, and organization transformation, a radical large-scale process that transforms the organization into something totally different.

It is clear that prisons in the United States are not rehabilitating offenders. The communication perspective examines the organization as it is through a study of language culture. Organization development provides means by which planned change can be implemented in organizational systems. Organization transformation is a systemwide process requiring all organization members to perceive, think, value, and behave in completely new ways, which radically alters the organization's controls, power centers, strategy, structure, vision, mission, goals, and objectives. The case is made that although organization development interventions and organizational communications analyses are useful for understanding the organization as it is and for planning change within the confines of the existing structure, they are not sufficient by themselves to address the most serious problems faced by prison organizations in the United States. It is suggested that due to its broadness of scope and radical nature, organization transformation theory may offer a new approach to the reconstruction of prisons as more effective organizations.

Prison Staff

The long-range goal of our study on prison staff is to understand the impact of staff attitudes on inmates and how they affect recidivism. In order to achieve this long-range purpose, this study examines specific staff attitudes and how they differ among staff members. The study discovered that the type of prior job held relates to attitudes toward the purpose of corrections; that is, those in treatment-related jobs are more likely to include rehabilitation in their definition of corrections and to have a definition that includes both corrections and rehabilitation than prison staff who have custodial positions, such as correctional officers (prison guards). One interesting finding that has implications for the state of Oklahoma is that staff members from Oklahoma are more likely to believe that the purpose of corrections is to punish offenders as opposed to rehabilitating them. The final phase of our research project involves designing programs for inmates that will enable them to successfully adjust to life outside of prison, thereby reducing recidivism. Programs to educate staff about the experience of women in prison and to train staff to assist inmates in their readjustment may be important to achieving this goal.

Communication

This chapter analyzes the language culture of staff and inmates. The author posits that analysis of language culture is one methodology that accesses the major dilemmas in correctional organizations. This study of a women's correctional organization is important because it provides insights into the reasons for the rising number of recidivating women. Using the concept that discourse is both spoken and written, the researcher analyzed the participants' discourse (e.g., written responses from surveys and audiotaped interviews) as indicative of correctional bureaucratic language culture. The language was analyzed by attention to what was said and how it was said. Perceptions about self, the correctional organization, purposes of corrections, and reasons for recidivism were analyzed as well as word choices, emphasis, and the descriptions that were used in responses. The analysis suggests that, in part through language, the co-optation of staff and inmates maintains the status quo and perpetuates the correctional organizational culture. The most important conclusion suggested by this study is that inmates who, through interaction with staff and other co-opted inmates, become emerged into the prison culture, are less suited to developing the skills and perspectives necessary to prevent their return to prison.

Theory Development

This study offers a theoretical frame by which to understand female crime and incarceration. In its exposition, Chapter 11 has relied on the concept of patriarchy at its conceptual core. In particular, it suggests that women's criminological experiences cannot be fully comprehended without first factoring in the importance of patriarchy as a defining characteristic of those experiences. Moreover, patriarchy emanates both privately and publicly in the lives of women. Often these expressions, though sharing the commonality of male oppression, are conflictual and contradictory. Much of the theoretical space in this analysis is devoted to understanding how the intersection of public and private patriarchy impact women's criminality. The discussion looks at public and private patriarchy as a structuring thread of criminal behavior among abused women; it examines the possible linkage between childhood abuse and later adult criminal behavior and how the characteristics of a community and the types of male associates interact to explain women's criminal behavior.

The process of surveillance as a principle in the construction of women as objects of discipline is also examined. This approach allows an escape from any patriarchal essentialism (i.e., the notion that all women are oppressed equally) while maintaining an integrated perspective on women's crime with an open patriarchy at its core. This study looks at how women are made objects of discipline by and through patriarchy and at how these expressions differ according to women's race, class, and physical appearance. Hence, it attempts to explain why some women are more likely to be arrested and incarcerated than others.

With respect to prison life, the study discusses power as a constitutive element in the construction of women's prison subculture, and the importance of class-specific sex-role socialization is briefly highlighted.

FUTURE RESEARCH

The findings reported in this book represent just a starting point for the analysis and dissemination of the large data base we have accumulated on imprisoned women in the state of Oklahoma. We have an extensive base of both qualitative and quantitative data from surveys and observations, and we will continue collecting more qualitative data through interviews and additional observations.

More research into women's crime is needed. Antiquated theories that explain female criminality by focusing on sexuality and stereotypical notions about women in general are no longer acceptable. There is a need for the development of new criminological theories that will reflect the reality of women's lives in prison. It is important to incorporate the notion of women's oppression as well as the unique challenges facing women in our society into new theories of female criminality.

Close scrutiny of existing prisons for women as well as a reevaluation of all facets of women's prisons are imperative in order to effectively intervene in the cycle of recidivism.

References

Adams, D., and Fisher, J. (1976). The effects of prison residents' community contacts on recidivism rates. *Corrective and Social Psychiatry*, *22*(4), 21–27.

Adams, J. (1984). *Transforming work*. Alexandria, VA: Miles River Press.

Adler, F. (1975). *Sisters in crime*. New York: McGraw-Hill.

Alexander, L. (1983). Retributivism and the inadvertent punishment of the innocent. *Law and Philosophy*, *2*, 233–34

American Correctional Association. (1990). *The female offender: What does the future hold?* Washington, DC: American Correctional Association.

American Friends Service Committee. (1990). *200 years of the penitentiary: Breaking chains, forging justice*. A special study. Philadelphia: American Friends Service Committee.

Amnesty International (1992, February). *United States of America: Death penalty developments in 1991*. London: International Secretariat.

Amsterdam, A. G. (1987, Winter). The Supreme Court and capital punishment. *Human Rights*, *14*, 14–70.

Atkinson, M., and Heritage, J. (1984). *Structures of social action: Studies in conversation analysis*. London: Cambridge University Press.

Auerbach, S. (1974). Common myths about capital criminals and their victims. *Georgia Journal of Corrections*, *3*(2), 41–54.

Bailey, W. C. (1991). The general prevention effect of capital punishment for non-capital felonies. In R. M. Bohm (Ed.), *The death penalty in America: Current research* (pp. 21–38). Cincinnati, OH: ACJS/Anderson.

Baker, J. E. (1985). *Prisoner participation in prison power*. Metuchen, NJ: Scarecrow Press.

Barfield, V. (1985). *Women on death row*. Nashville: Oliver-Nelson Books.

Barry, E. (1987, Winter). Imprisoned mothers face extra hardships. *National Prison Project Journal*, *14*, 20–25.

Bartky, S. (1992). Foucault, femininity, and the modernization of patriarchal power. In J. Kourany, J. Sterban, and R. Tong (Eds.), *Feminist philosophies* (pp. 103–18). Englewood Cliffs, NJ: Prentice Hall.

Baum, H. (1987). *The invisible bureaucracy: The unconscious in organization problem solving.* New York: Oxford University Press.

Baunach, P. J. (1982). You can't be a mother in prison—can you? Impact of the mother-child separation. In Price, B. R. and Sokoloff, N. (Eds.), *Criminal justice system and women* (pp. 155–69). New York: Clark Boardman.

Bauschard, L., and Kimbrough, M. (1986). *Voices set free: Battered women speak from prison.* St. Louis, MO: Women's Self-Help Center.

Becker, H. (1963). *Outsiders: Studies in the sociology of deviance.* New York: Free Press.

Bedau, H. A. (1982). *The death penalty in America* (3rd ed.). New York: Oxford University Press.

Bedau, H. A. (1984). *The case against the death penalty.* Washington, DC: American Civil Liberties Union.

Bennett, L. A. (1974). Self-esteem and parole adjustment. *Criminology, 12* (3), 346–60.

Benokraitis, N. V., and Feagin, J. R. (1986). *Modern sexism.* Englewood Cliffs, NJ: Simon and Schuster.

Benson, D. E., and Mullins, E. (1990). Consistency of role identity and self-esteem. *National Journal of Sociology, 4*(2), 159–173.

Billig, M., Condor, S., Edwards, D., Gene, M., Middleton, D., and Radley, A. (1988). *Ideological dilemmas: A social psychology of everyday thinking.* Beverly Hills, CA: Sage.

Billingsley, A. (1968). *Black families in white America.* Englewood Cliffs, NJ: Prentice Hall.

Blackwell, J. E. (1991). *The black community: Diversity and unity.* New York: HarperCollins.

Blau, P. (1974). *On the nature of organizations.* New York: Wiley.

Blummer, H. (1969). *Symbolic interactionism: Perspective and method.* Englewood Cliffs, NJ: Prentice Hall.

Bolman, L. G., and Deal, T. E. (1984). *Modern approaches to understanding and managing organizations.* San Francisco: Jossey-Bass.

Bowker, L. H. (1978). *Prisons and prisoners: A bibliographic guide.* San Francisco: R. & E. Research Associates.

Broverman, I., Vogel, S., Broverman, D., Clarkson, F., and Rosenkrantz, P. (1972). Sex-role stereotypes: A current appraisal. *Journal of Social Issues, 28,* 59–78.

Brown, A. (1989). *When battered women kill.* NY: Free Press.

Bureau of the Census. (1992). Housing summary tape 5. File 1-A. Washington, DC: U.S. Government Printing Office.

Bureau of Justice Statistics. (1987). *Recidivism of young parolees.* (Report No. NCJ–104916). Washington, DC: U.S. Department of Justice, Bureau of Justice Statistics.

Bureau of Justice Statistics. (1988a). *BJS data report, 1987*. (Report No. NCJ–110643). Washington, DC: U.S. Department of Justice, Bureau of Justice Statistics.

Bureau of Justice Statistics. (1988b). *Profile of state prison inmates, 1986*. (Report No. NCJ–109926). Washington, DC: U.S. Department of Justice, Bureau of Justice Statistics.

Bureau of Justice Statistics. (1989a). *Capital punishment, 1988*. (Report No. NCJ–118313). Washington, DC: U.S. Department of Justice, Bureau of Justice Statistics.

Bureau of Justice Statistics. (1989b). *Recidivism of prisoners released in 1983*. (Report No. NCJ–116261). Washington, DC: U. S. Department of Justice, Bureau of Justice Statistics.

Bureau of Justice Statistics. (1990a). *Capital punishment, 1989*. (Report No. NCJ–124545). Washington, DC: U.S. Department of Justice, Bureau of Justice Statistics.

Bureau of Justice Statistics. (1990b). *Sourcebook of criminal justice statistics, 1989*. (Report No. J29.9/6:990). Washington, DC: U.S. Department of Justice, Bureau of Justice Statistics.

Bureau of Justice Statistics. (1991a). *Correctional populations in the United States, 1988*. (Report No. NCJ–124280). Washington, DC: U.S. Department of Justice, Bureau of Justice Statistics.

Bureau of Justice Statistics. (1991b). *Correctional populations in the United States, 1989*. (Report No. NCJ–130445). Washington, DC: U.S. Department of Justice, Bureau of Justice Statistics.

Bureau of Justice Statistics. (1991c). *Implications of the drug use forecasting data for FASC programs: Female arrestees*. (Report No. NCJ–129671). Washington, DC: U.S. Department of Justice, Bureau of Justice Statistics.

Bureau of Justice Statistics. (1991d). *National update, 1*(1). (Report No. NCJ–129863). Washington, DC: U.S. Department of Justice, Bureau of Justice Statistics.

Bureau of Justice Statistics. (1991e). *Prisoners in 1990*. (Report No. NCJ–129198). Washington, DC: U.S. Department of Justice, Bureau of Justice Statistics.

Bureau of Justice Statistics. (1991f). *Special report: Women in prison*. (Report No. NCJ–127991). Washington, DC: U.S. Department of Justice, Bureau of Justice Statistics.

Bureau of Justice Statistics. (1991g). *Violent crime in the United States*. (Report No. NCJ–127855). Washington, DC: U.S. Department of Justice, Bureau of Justice Statistics

Burke, K. (1966). *Language as symbolic action*. Berkeley, CA: University of California Press.

Burrell, G., and Morgan, G. (1979). *Sociological paradigms and organizational analysis*. New York: Heinemann.

Burstein, J. (1977). *Conjugal visits in prison*. Lexington, MA: Lexington Books.

Butler, S. (1978). *Conspiracy of silence: The trauma of incest.* San Francisco: New Glide Publications.

Capital punishment. (1976, July 10). *The Saturday Oklahoman and Times*, p. 1.

Carlen, P., and Worrall, A. (Eds.). (1987). *Gender, crime and justice.* Philadelphia: Open University Press.

Center for the Study of Crime, Delinquency, and Social Control. (1988, December). Attitudes of Oklahomans toward the death penalty. Control Study 8802. Norman, OK: University of Oklahoma.

Chesney-Lind, M. (1978). Young women in the arms of the law. In L. Bowker (Ed.), *Women, crime, and the criminal justice system* (pp. 171–96). Lexington, MA: Lexington Books.

Chodorow, N. (1978). *The reproduction of mothering.* Berkeley, CA: University of California Press.

Citizens United for Rehabilitation of Errants. (1992, Winter). *Cure.* (Newsletter). Washington, DC,

Clay, N. (1988, March 12). City woman charged in deaths. *Oklahoma Times,* pp. 1–2.

Clayton, R. R., Voss, H. L., Robbins, C., and Skinner, W. F. (1987). Gender differences in drug use: An epidemiological perspective. In B. A. Ray and M. C. Braude (Eds.), *National institute of drug abuse research monograph, series 65* (pp. 80–99). (DHS Pub. No. ADM 87–1447). Washington, DC: U.S. Government Printing Office.

Clemmer, D. (1958). *The prison community.* New York: Rinehart

Colten, M. E. (1979). A description and comparative analysis of self-perceptions and attitudes of heroin-addicted women. In Department of Health, Education and Welfare (DHEW, Ed.), *Addicted women: Family dynamics, self perceptions, and support systems.* (DHEW Pub. No. ADM 80–762). Rockville, MD: National Institute on Drug Abuse.

Coontz, P. D. (1983). Women under sentence of death: The social organization of waiting to die. *Prison Journal, 63*(2), 88–98.

Cressey, D. (1965). Prison organizations. In J. G. March (Ed.), *Handbook of organizations* (pp. 1023–1070). Chicago: Rand McNally.

Culpepper, L. (1991, October 30). Violence at home. *The Oklahoma Daily.* University of Oklahoma Publications.

Cummings, H. W., Long, L. W., and Lewis, M. (1987). *Managing communication in organizations: An introduction* (2nd ed.). Scottsdale, AZ: Gorsuch Scarisbrick.

Cummings, T. G., and Huse, E. F. (1989). *Organizational development and change* (4th ed.). St. Paul, MN: West Publishing.

Cyert, R., and March, J. (1963). *A behavioral theory of the firm.* Englewood Cliffs, NJ: Prentice Hall.

Davis, P. C. (1978). Texas capital sentencing procedures: The role of the jury and the restraining hand of the expert. *Journal of Criminal Law and Criminology, 69,* 300–10.

DeSola, R. E. (1988). *Crime dictionary.* New York: Facts on File Publications.

de Young, M. (Ed.). (1987). *Child molestation: An annotated bibliography.* Jefferson, NC: Mc Farland.

Dooley, D. (1990). *Social research methods* (2nd ed.) Englewood Cliffs, NJ: Prentice Hall.

Dukes, R. L. and Lorch, B. D. (1989). The effects of school, family, self-concept, and deviant behavior on adolescent suicide ideation. *Journal of Adolescence, 12,* 239–51.

Durkheim, E. (1933). *The division of labor in society.* New York: Free Press.

Durkheim, E. (1964). *The rules of sociological method.* London: Free Press. (original work published in 1895).

Facts on File (1992, February 20), *52* (2674), 113–14.

File, K. N. (1976). Sex roles and street roles. *International Journal of the Addictions, 11,* 263–68.

Finhelhorn, D., and Browne, A. (1985, October). The traumatic impact of child sexual abuse: A conceptualization. *American Journal of Orthopsychiatry, 55*(4), 520–41.

Fitch, G. (1970). Effects of self-esteem, perceived performance and choice on causal attributions. *Journal of personality and Social Psychology, 16,* 311–15.

Fletcher, B. R. (1990). *Organization transformation theorists and practitioners: Profiles and themes.* New York: Praeger.

Fletcher, B. R. (1992). Human relations 5100: Organization transformation. (Lecture notes). Norman: University of Oklahoma.

Fletcher, B. R., Moon, D., and Rolison, G. (1992). Project for recidivism research and female inmate training. Unpublished paper presented at the 1992 Academy of Criminal Justice Sciences Meeting.

Fletcher, B. R., Shaver, L. D., and Moon, D. G. (1991). Profile: The female inmate. A conference paper presented at the Fourth National Workshop on Women Offenders, Washington, DC.

Foster, L. A., Veale, C. M., and Fogel, C. J. (1989). Factors present when battered women kill. *Issues in Mental Health Nursing, 10,* 273–84.

Foucault, M. (1977). *Discipline and punish: The birth of the prison.* London: Penguin Press.

Fox, J. G. (1982). *Organizational and racial conflict in maximum-security prisons.* Lexington, MA: Lexington Books.

Frankel, M. C. (1973). *Criminal sentences: Law without order.* New York: Hill and Wang.

Frankel, R. (1984). From sentence to "sequence": Understanding the medical encounter through microinteractional analysis. *Discourse Analysis, 7,* 135–70.

French, L. (1978). *Women, crime and the male-dominated criminal justice system.* Washington, DC: U.S. Department of Health, Education, and Welfare.

Furman v. Georgia. (1972). 408 U.S. 241–312 (pp. 2727–2763).

Galtung, J. (1961). Prison: The organization of dilemma. In D. Cressey (Ed.), *The prison: Studies in institutional organization and change* (pp. 107–45). New York: Holt, Rinehart, and Winston.

Garrity, D. L. (1961). The prison as a rehabilitative agency. In D. Cressey (Ed), *The prison: Studies in institutional organizations and change* (pp. 358–80). New York: Holt, Rinehart, and Winston.

Geertz, C. (1973). *The interpretation of cultures.* New York: Basic Books.

Genders, E., and Player, E. (1987). Women in prison: The treatment, the control, and the experience. In P. Carlen and A. Worrall (Eds.), *Gender, crime and justice* (pp. 161–75). Philadelphia: Open University Press.

Gendreau, P., Grant, B. A., and Leipciger, M. (1979). Self-esteem, incarceration and recidivism. *Criminal Justice and Behavior, 6*(1), 67–75.

Genovese, E. (1976). *Roll Jordan roll: the world the slaves made.* New York: Vintage Books.

Giallombardo, R. (1966). *Society of women: A study of a women's prison.* New York: Wiley.

Giddens, A. (1979). *Central problems in social theory.* Berkeley: University of California Press.

Glaser, D. (1969). *The effectiveness of a prison and parole system* (Abridged Ed.). Indianapolis: Bobb-Merrill.

Glenn, L. (1990). Health care communication between American Indian women and a white male doctor: A study of interaction at a public health care facility. Ph.D. diss., University of Oklahoma.

Goffman, E. (1961a). *Asylums.* Chicago: Aldine Press.

Goffman, E. (1961b). On the characteristics of total institutions: The inmate world. In D. Cressey (Ed.), *The prison: Studies in institutional organization and change* (pp. 15–67). New York: Holt, Rinehart, and Winston.

Goffman, E. (1963). *Stigma: Notes on the management of spoiled identity.* Englewood Cliffs, NJ: Prentice Hall.

Goldsmith, H. R., Jr. (1987). Self-esteem of juvenile delinquents: Findings and implications. *Journal of Offender Counseling, 11*(2), 79–85.

Goodstein, L., and Wright, K. (1989). Inmate adjustment to prison. In L. Goodstein and D. MacKenzie (Eds.). *The American prison* (pp. 229–52). New York: Plenum.

Gora, J. G. (1982). *The new female criminal.* New York: Praeger.

Griswold, H. J. (1971). *An eye for an eye.* New York: Pocket Books.

Gross, S. R., and Mauro, R. (1983, November). Patterns of death: An analysis of racial disparities in capital sentencing and homicide victimization. *Stanford Law Review, 37,* 27–153.

Grupp, S. E. (1971). *Theories of punishment.* Bloomington: Indiana University Press.

Hairston, C. F. (1991). Family ties during imprisonment: Important to whom and for what? *Corrective and Social Psychiatry, 22*(4), 21–27.

Hall, E. (1966). *The hidden dimension.* New York: Random House.

Hall, S., Critcher, C., Jefferson, T., Clarke, J., and Roberts, B. (1978). *Policing the crisis, mugging, the state and law and order*. London: Macmillan.

Haney, C. (1984). On selection of capital juries: The biasing effects of the death-qualification process. *Law and Human Behavior, 8*, 121–32.

Hannum, T. E., Borgan, F. H., and Anderson, R. M. (1978). Self-concept changes associated with incarceration in female prisoners. *Criminal Justice and Behavior, 5*(3), 271–79.

Hansen, J. O. (1992, April 26). Is justice taking a beating? *The Atlanta Constitution*, pp. A1–A7.

Hanson, M. (1991). Alcoholism and other addictions. In A. Gitterman (Ed.), *Handbook of social work practice with vulnerable populations* (pp. 65–100). New York: Columbia University Press.

Harman, W. (1988). *Global mind change: The promise of the last years of the twentieth century*. Indianapolis: Institute of Noetic Sciences Knowledge Systems.

Harris, A. (1977). Age, sex and the versatility of delinquent involvements. *American Sociological Review, 42* (February), 3–18.

Harrison, B., Guy, R. F., and Lupfer, S. L. (1981). Locus of control and self-esteem as correlates of role orientation in traditional and nontraditional women. *Sex roles, 7*(12), 1175–1187.

Hartinger, W., Eldefonso, E., and Coffey, A. (1973). *Corrections: A component of the criminal justice system*. Pacific Palisades, CA: Goodyear.

Hawton, K. (1986). *Suicide and attempted suicide among children and adolescents*. Beverly Hills: Sage.

Heidensohn, F. (1985). *Women and crime*. New York: New York University Press.

Hendin, H. (1985). Suicide among the youth: Psychodynamics and demography. In M. L. Peck, R. E. Farberow, and R. E. Litman (Eds.), *Youth suicide*. New York: Springer.

Hepburn, J. R., and Albonetti, C. (1980). Role conflict in correctional institutions: An empirical examination of the treatment-custody dilemma among correctional staff. *Criminology, 17*(4), 445–59.

Herman, J. L., Perry, C., and Van der Kolk, B. A. (1989). Childhood trauma in borderline personality disorder. *American Journal of Psychiatry, 146*(4), 490–95.

Hoffman-Bustamante, D. (1973). The nature of female criminality. *Issues in Criminology, 8* (Fall), 117–36.

Hogarth, J. (1971). *Sentencing as a human process*. Toronto: University of Toronto Press.

Holt, N., and Miller, D. (1972). *Explorations in inmate-family relationships*. Sacramento, CA: California Department of Corrections.

Hummel, R. (1987). *The bureaucratic experience* (3rd ed.). New York: St. Martin's.

Irwin, J. (1970). *The felon*. Englewood Cliffs, NJ: Prentice Hall.

Jablin, F., Putnam, L., Roberts, K., and Porter, L. (Eds.). (1987). *Handbook of organizational communication: An interdisciplinary perspective.* Beverly Hills, CA: Sage.

Jackson, D. B., Carter, V., and Rolison, G. L. (1992). Profile of the minority female offender. Paper presented at the Academy of Criminal Justice Sciences annual conference, Pittsburgh, PA.

Jensen, V. (1991). *Convicts, residents, and inmates: Social types in a women's prison.* M.A. thesis, University of Oklahoma.

Johnson, R. (1980). Warehousing for death: Observations on the human environment of death row. *Crime and Delinquency, 26,* 545–62.

Judson, C. J., Pandell, J. J., Owens, J. B., McIntosh, J. L., and Matschullat, D. L. (1969). A study of the California jury in first-degree murder cases. *Stanford Law Review, 21,* 1297–1437.

Kalinich, D. B., and Pitcher, T. (1984). *Surviving in corrections: A guide for corrections professionals.* Springfield, IL: Charles C. Thomas.

Kaplan, S. M. (1985, July). Death, so say we all. *Psychology Today,* pp. 48–53.

Katz, D., and Kahn, R. (1966). *The social psychology of organizations.* New York: Wiley.

Kauffman, K. (1988). *Prison officers and their world.* Cambridge, MA: Harvard University Press.

Kelley, H. (1972). *Attribution: Perceiving the causes of behavior.* Morristown, NJ: General Learning Press.

Kleck, G. (1981). Racial discrimination in criminal sentencing. *American Sociological Review, 46,* 783–804.

Klein, D. (1982). The etiology of female crime: A review of the literature. In B. R. Price and N. J Sokoloff (Eds.), *The criminal justice system and women: Offenders, victims, and workers* (pp. 35–60). New York: Clark Bourdman.

Knowlton, R. C. (1953). Problems of jury discretion in capital cases. *University of Pennsylvania Law Review, 101,* 1099–1136.

Koban, L. A. (1983). Parents in prison: A comparative analysis of the effects of incarceration on the families of men and women. *Research in Law, Deviance, and Social Control, 5,* 171–83.

Kreps, G. (1990). Organizational communication research and organizational development. In D. O'Hair and G. Kreps (Eds.), *Applied communication theory and research* (pp. 103–25). Hillsdale, NJ: Lawrence Erlbaum.

Kroll, M. A. (1987). Death watch: Counsel for the condemned. *California Lawyer, 24-7* (December), 106–9.

Kruttschnitt, C. (1982). Women, crime, and dependency: An application of the theory of law. *Criminology, 19,* 495–513.

Lacayo, R. (1992, June 1). You don't always get Perry Mason. *Time Magazine,* pp. 38–39.

Lambert, L. R., and Madden, P. G. (1976, October). The adult female offender; the road from institution to community life. *Canadian Journal of Criminology and Corrections, 18*(4), 319–31.

Larson, J. H., and Nelson, J. (1984). Women friendship and adaptation to prison. *Journal of Criminal Justice, 12*(4), 601–15.

LeFlore, L., and Holston, M. A. (1989). Perceived importance of parenting behaviors as reported by inmate mothers: An exploratory study. *Journal of Offender Counseling, Services, and Rehabilitation, 13*(1), 5–21.

Leonard, E. B. (1982). *A critique of criminological theory: Women, crime, and society.* New York: Longman.

Levy, A., and Merry, U. (1986). *Organizational transformation: Approaches, strategies, theories.* New York: Praeger.

Lewin, K. (1947). Psychology and the process of group living. *Journal of Social Psychology, 17,* 119–29.

Lewis, P. W., Mannle, H. W., Allen, H. E., and Vetter, H. J. (1979). A post-Furman profile of Florida's condemned: A question of discrimination in terms of the race of the victim and a comment on Spenkellink v. Wainwright. *Stetson Law Review, 9,* 1–45.

Littlejohn, S. W. (1989). *Theories of human communication* (3rd ed.). Belmont, CA: Wadsworth.

Love, G. D. (1991). Consideration of the inmate student's locus of control for effective instructional leadership. *Journal of Correctional Education, 42*(1), 36–41.

Mackey, P. E. (1976). *Voices against death: American opposition to capital punishment, 1787–1975.* New York: Burt Franklin.

Mandaraka-Sheppard, A. (1986). *The dynamics of aggression in women's prisons in England.* London: Gower.

Mann, C. R. (1984). *Female crime and delinquency.* Huntsville: University of Alabama.

Martin, Jr., G. T. (1990). *Social policy in the welfare state.* Englewood Cliffs, NJ: Prentice Hall.

Martin, R. L., Cloniger, R., and Guze, S. B. (1978, February). Female criminality and the prediction of recidivism: A prospective six-year follow-up. *Archives of General Psychiatry, 35*(2), 207–14.

Masur, L. P. (1989). *Rites of execution: Capital punishment and transformation of American culture.* New York: Oxford University Press.

Mayo, E. (1960). *The social problems of an industrial civilization.* New York: Viking.

McCall, J. G., and Simmons, J. L. (1978). *Identities and interactions: An examination of human association in everyday life* (rev. ed.). New York: Free Press.

McCleery, R. H. (1961). The governmental process and informal social control. In D. Cressey (Ed.), *The prison: Studies in institutional organizations and change* (pp. 149–88). New York: Holt, Rinehart, and Winston.

McCorkle, L., and Korn, R. (1954). Resocialization within walls. *Annals of the American Academy of Political Science, 239,* 88–98.

McCracken, G. (1988). *The long interview.* Newbury Park, CA: Sage.

McGowan, B. G., and Blumenthal, K. L. (1978). *Why punish the children? A study of children of women prisoners.* Washington, DC: National Council on Crime and Delinquency.

McGregor, D. (1960). *The human side of enterprise.* New York: McGraw-Hill.

Mead, G. (1934). *Mind, self and society.* Chicago: University of Chicago Press.

Mecoy, D. (1988, August 30). Wife arrested in death of man found in pick-up. *Oklahoma Times*, pp. 1, 4.

Menninger, K. (1968). *The crime of punishment.* New York: Viking.

Merton, R. K. (1957). *Social theory and social structure.* New York: Free Press.

Middendorff, W. (1971). Untitled. In H. Hart (Ed.), *Punishment: For and against* (pp. 10–38). New York: Hart.

Miller, D. (1990). Women in pain: Substance abuse/self-medication. In M. P. Mirkin (Ed.), *The social and political contexts of family therapy* (pp. 179–92). Boston: Allyn and Bacon.

Moon, D. G. (1990). *How the study of women has impacted women in prison.* Unpublished paper. Norman: University of Oklahoma.

Moon, D. G. (1991). Transforming prison organizations. Unpublished paper. Norman, OK: University of Oklahoma.

Moreman, M. (1988). *Talking culture: Ethnography and conversation analysis.* Philadelphia: University of Pennsylvania Press.

Morris, A. (1987). *Women, crime and criminal justice.* New York: Basil Blackwell.

Murton, T. (1969). Treatment of condemned prisoners. *Crime and Delinquency, 15,* 94–111.

NAACP Legal Defense and Education Fund, Inc. (NAACP). (1992, Spring). *Death row, U.S.A. summary.* New York: National Office of NAACP Legal Defense Fund.

NAACP Legal Defense and Education Fund, Inc. (NAACP). (1982, Spring). *Death row, U.S.A. summary.* New York: National Office of NAACP Legal Defense Fund.

National Coalition to Abolish the Death Penalty. (1992, March). *Women on death row.* Washington, DC: National Coalition to Abolish the Death Penalty.

National Institute of Corrections. (1991, July). *Intervening with substance-abusing offenders: A framework of action.* (Report No. 296–934/40539). Washington, DC: U.S. Government Printing Office.

National Institute on Drug Abuse. (1991). *National household survey on drug abuse: Population estimates 1990.* Washington, DC: U.S. Government Printing Office.

Nettler, G. (1982). *Responding to crime.* Cincinnati, OH: Anderson.

Newman, D. J. (1975). *Introduction to criminal justice.* New York: Lippincott.

Newman, G. (1978). *The punishment response.* New York: Lippincott.

O'Donnell, P., Churgin, M. J., and Curtis, D. E. (1977). *Toward a just and effective sentencing system: Agenda for legislative reform.* New York: Praeger.

O'Hair, D., and Kreps, G. (1983). *Communication and organizations: An interpretive approach*. Newbury Park, CA: Sage.

Oklahoma Department of Correction. (1989). Female offender task force report. Unpublished draft. Oklahoma City, OK.

Oklahoma Department of Corrections. (1991, February). Estimated percent of females with prior receptions for fiscal years 1980 to 1990. Unpublished report. Oklahoma City, OK.

Orlofsky, S., Bank, M., and Hitchings, T. E. (1985, February 15). *Facts on file yearbook: The indexed record of world events*, *45*(2308), p. 123E1.

O'Shea, K. (1992). Interview with woman on death row. Raw data for Project for Recidivism Research and Female Inmate Training. Norman: University of Oklahoma.

Otterbein, K. F. (1986). *The ultimate coercive sanction: A cross-cultural study of capital punishment*. New Haven, CT: HRAF.

Owen, H. (1987). *Spirit: Transformation and development in organizations*. Potomac, MD: Abbott.

Packer, H. (1971). Justifications for criminal punishment. In E. J. MacNamara and E. S. Sagarin (Eds.), *Perspectives on correction* (pp. 98–125). New York: Thomas Crowell.

Parisi, N. (1982). Are families treated differently? A review of theories and evidence on sentencing and parole decisions. In N. H. Rafter and E. A. Stanko (Eds.), *Judge, lawyer, victim, thief* (pp. 38–52). Boston: Northeastern University Press.

Paternoster, R. (1983). Race of victim and location of crime: The decision to seek the death penalty in South Carolina. *Journal of Criminal Law and Criminology*, *74*, 754–85.

Pollack-Byrne, J. M. (1990). *Women, prison, and crime*. Belmont, CA: Brooks/Cole.

Pondy, L., Fronst, P., Morgan, G., and Dandridge, T. (Eds.). (1983). *Organizational symbolism*. Greenwich, CT: JAI Press.

Potter, J., and Wetherell, M. (1987). *Discourse and social psychology: Beyond attitudes and behavior*. Beverly Hills, CA: Sage.

Project for Recidivism Research and Female Inmate Training (PRRFIT). (1991). Raw unpublished data. Norman: University of Oklahoma.

Pugliesi, K. (1989). Social support and self-esteem as intervening variables in the relationship between social roles and women's well-being. *Community Mental Health Journal*, *25*(2), 87–100.

Putnam, L., and Pacanowsky, M. (1983). *Communication and organizations: An interpretive approach*. Beverly Hills, CA: Sage.

Rabinow, P., and Sullivan, W. (Eds.). (1979). *Interpretive social science: A reader*. Berkeley: University of California Press.

Radelet, M. L., and Bedau, H. A. (1988). Fallibility and finality: Type II errors on capital punishment. In K. C. Haas and J. A. Inciardi (Eds.), *Challenging capital punishment: Legal and social science approaches* (pp. 70–85). Newbury Park, CA: Sage.

Radelet, M. L., and Pierce, G. L. (1985). Race and prosecutorial discretion in homicide cases. *Law and Society Review*, *19*, 587–621.

Randall-David, E. (1990). *Women helping women: Networks for support and caring*. Washington, DC: The Maternal and Child Health Clearing-house.

Rawls, J. (1971). *A theory of justice*. Cambridge, MA: Cambridge Press.

Ray, B. A., and Braude, M. C. (1987). Women and drugs: A new era for research. *In National institute on drug abuse research monograph series 65*. (DHS Pub. No. ADM 37–1447). Washington, DC: U.S. Government Printing Office.

Reed, B. G. (1985). Intervention strategies for drug-dependent women: An introduction. In G. M. Beschner, G. G. Reed, and J. Mondanaro (Eds.), *Treatment services for drug-dependent women*, *1*, (pp. 1-24). (DHHS Pub. No. ADM 35–1177). Rockville, MD: National Institute on Drug Abuse.

Ricoeur, P. (1991). The model of the text: Meaningful action considered as text. In P. Ricoeur (Ed.), *From the text to action: Essays in hermeneutics, II* (trans. K. Blamey and J. Thompson, pp. 144–167). Evanston, IL: North-western University Press.

Rolison, G. L (1992). *Reliability and validity*. Unpublished manuscript. Norman: University of Oklahoma.

Rosenberg, F., and Rosenberg, M. (1978). Self-esteem and delinquency. *Journal of Youth and Adolescence*, *7*, 279–91.

Rosewater, L. B. (1985). Schizophrenic, borderline, or battered? In L. B. Rosewater and L. E. Walker (Eds.), *Handbook of feminist therapy* (pp. 215–25). New York: Springer.

Ross, R. R., and Fabiano, E. A. (1986). *Female offenders: Correctional afterthoughts*. Jefferson, NC: McFarland.

Russell, D.E.H. (1983). The incidence and prevalence of intrafamilial and extrafamilial sexual abuse of female children. *Child Abuse and Neglect*, *7*(2), 133–46.

Ryckman, R., and Sherman, M. (1973). Relationship between self-esteem and internal-external locus of control. *Psychological Reports*, *32*, 1106ff.

Sales, E., Baun, M., and Shore, B. (1984). Victim readjustment following assault. *Journal of Social Issues*, *40*(1), 117–36.

Sanford, L. T., and Donovan, M. E. (1984). *Women and self-esteem*. New York: Viking Penguin.

Sarat, A., and Vidmar, N. (1976). Public opinion: The death penalty and the eighth amendment: Testing the Marshall hypothesis. *Wisconsin Law Review*, *17*, 171–206.

Schneider, V., and Smykla, J. O. (1991). A summary analysis of executions in the United States, 1608–1987: The espy file. In R. M. Bohm (Ed.), *The death penalty in America: Current research* (pp. 1–19). Cincinnati, OH: Anderson.

Schmittroth, L. (Ed.). (1991). *Statistical record of women worldwide*. Detroit: Gale Research.

Schrag, C. (1961). Some foundations for a theory of correction. In D. Cressey (Ed.), *The prison: Studies in institutional organizations and change* (pp. 309–57). New York: Holt, Rinehart, and Winston.

Shaver, P., and Shaver L. (1992). Signs in the organization: Architectural changes as organizational rhetoric in a public health facility. Paper presented to Western States Communication Association, Boise, ID.

Simon, H. (1945). *Administrative behavior*. New York: Macmillan.

Simon, R. (1975). *The contemporary woman and crime*. Rockville, MD: National Institute of Mental Health, Crime and Delinquency Issues.

Singh, U. P (1970). The self-concept of both criminal male and female: A comparative study. *Psychological Studies*, *15*, 101–7.

Smircich, L., and Calas, M. (1987). Organizational culture: A critical assessment. In F. Jablin, L. Putnam, K. Roberts, and L. Porter (Eds.). *Handbook of organizational communication: An interdisciplinary perspective* (pp. 228–63). Beverly Hills, CA: Sage.

Solomon, J. (1988). *The signs of our times: Semiotics: The hidden messages of environment, objects, and cultural images*. Los Angeles: Tarcher.

Sorenson, J. R., and Marquart, J. W. (1989). Working the dead. In M. L. Radelet (Ed.), *Facing the death penalty: Essays on a cruel and unusual punishment* (pp. 169–77). Philadelphia: Temple University Press.

Steffensmeier, D. J. (1980). Assessing the impact of the women's movement on sex-based differences in the handling of adult criminal defendants. *Crime and Delinquency*, *26*(3), 18–24.

Streib, V. L. (1991, March). *Capital punishment for female offenders: Present female death row inmates and death sentences and executions of female offenders, January 1, 1973, to March 1, 1991*. Cleveland: Cleveland State University Press.

Sutker, P. B. (1985). Drug-dependent women. In U.S. Department of Health and Human Services (Ed.), *Treatment services for drug-dependent women* (pp. 25–51). (DHHS Pub. No. ADM 85–1177). Washington, DC: U.S. Government Printing Office.

Suval, E. M., and Brisson, R. C. (1974). Neither beauty nor beast: Female criminal homicide offenders. *International Journal of Criminology and Penology*, *2*, 23–34.

Sykes, G. (1958). *The society of captives*. Princeton, NJ: Princeton University Press.

Sypher, B., Applegate, J., and Sypher, H. (1985). Culture and communication in organizational contexts. In W. B. Gudykundst, L. Stewart, and S. Ting-Toomey (Eds.), *Communication, culture, and organizational process* (pp. 13–29). Newbury Park, CA: Sage.

Tahlequah man, mother charged in shooting death. (1982, July 6). *Oklahoma Times*, p. 4.

Taylor, F. (1911). *Scientific management*. New York: Harper.

Thompson, K. M. (1989). Effects of early alcohol use on adolescents' relations with peers and self-esteem: Patterns over time. *Adolescence, 24*(96), 837–49.

Tittle, C. (1973). Institutional living and self-esteem. *Social Problems, 20*(4), 65–77.

Trafford, A. (1991, February 26). Why battered women kill: Self-defense, not revenge, is often the motive. *Washington Post*, pp. A3, B7.

U.S. National Commission on the Causes and Prevention of Violence. (1971). National violence commission report. In L. Radzinowicz and M. E. Wolfgang (Eds.), *The criminal in society* (pp. 255–80). New York: Basic Books.

Walby, S. (1990). *Theorizing patriarchy*. Cambridge, MA: Basil Blackwell.

Walker, L. E. (1984). *The battered woman syndrome*. New York: Springer.

Ward, D., and Kassebaum, B. (1965). *Women's prison: Sex and social structure*. Chicago: Aldine.

Weber, M. (1947). *The theory of social and economic organization*. (Trans. A. M. Henderson and T. Parson). New York: Oxford University Press.

Weber, M. (1968). *Economy and society*. Berkeley: University of California Press.

Werth, P. (1981). The concept of "relevance": In conversational analysis. In P. Werth (Ed.), *Conversation and discourse: Structure and interpretation* (pp. 229–54). New York: St. Martin's.

Wheeler, S. (1961). Role conflict in correctional communities. In D. Cressey (Ed.), *The prison: Studies in institutional organizations and change* (pp. 229–59). New York: Holt, Rinehart, and Winston.

Whinery, L. H. (1976). *Predictive sentencing*. Lexington, MA: D. C. Heath.

Widom, C. S. (1979). Three assumptions about self-esteem, sex-role identity, and feminism. *Criminal Justice and Behavior, 6*(4), 365–82.

Widom, C. S. (1991). The role of placement experiences in mediating the criminal consequences of early childhood victimization. *American Journal of Orthopsychiatry, 61*(2), 195–209.

Williams, V. L. (1979). *Dictionary of American Penology*. Westport, CT: Greenwood.

Williamson, H. E. (1990). *The corrections profession*. Newbury Park, CA: Sage.

Wolfgang, M. E., and Riedel, M. (1973). Race, judicial discretion, and the death penalty. *The Annals of the American Academy of Political and Social Science, 407*, 119–33.

Worrall, A. (1989). Working with female offenders: Beyond alternatives to custody. *British Journal of Social Work, 19*, 77–93.

Worrall, A. (1990). *Offending women: Female lawbreakers and the criminal justice system*. London: Routledge.

Zalman, M. (1976). *Indeterminate sentencing laws: Present, past, and future*. Dallas, TX: Academy of Criminal Justice Sciences.

Zeisel, H. (1981). Race bias in the administration of the death penalty: The Florida experience. *Harvard Law Review, 95,* 456–68.

Zimring, F. E., and Hawkins, G. (1986). *Capital punishment and the American agenda.* New York: Cambridge University Press.

Index

Index

About the Contributors

REGINA BENNETT is a feminist who has held positions at shelters for battered women, rape crisis centers, a halfway house, a prison, a women's bookstore, and a fair housing center. She is currently studying for a doctorate in English literature at the University of Oklahoma.

LISA J. BILLY, a Native American of the Chickasaw and Choctaw nations, is a graduate student at the University of Oklahoma. She is an artist, educator, administrator, and innovator. Ms. Billy has won numerous awards and has exhibited award-winning art throughout the United States. She is the founding director of "Peacemakers," a nationally recognized organization for motivating Indian youth.

DEBORAH BINKLEY-JACKSON is an African American with a master's degree in Human Relations from the University of Oklahoma. Her professional background includes facilitating workshops in multicultural awareness and intra/interpersonal relations skills for both male and female inmates, victims of criminal activities, high school students, and university students.

VIVIAN L. CARTER is a University of Oklahoma doctoral candidate in the Department of Sociology and an active advocate for women, minorities, and children. She is a member of Delta Sigma Theta sorority, National Black Graduate Students Association, and the National Association of Graduate and Professional Students.

BEVERLY R. FLETCHER is Assistant Professor of Human Relations at the University of Oklahoma and specializes in organization transformation and development concepts, processes, and applications. Professor Fletcher is cofounder and co–principal investigator of the Project for Recidivism Research and Female Inmate Training, which involves action research in Oklahoma state correctional facilities for female offenders. Her doctorate in Organization Development is from the School of Education at the University of Massachusetts. In 1990 Dr. Fletcher published a book, *Organization Transformation Theorists and Practitioners: Profiles and Themes* (Praeger).

CONSTANCE HARDESTY is an Assistant Professor at the University of Oklahoma, Department of Sociology. Her Ph.D. in Sociology is from the University of Kentucky. She is a member of the American Sociological Association, National Council on Family Relations, and the Rural Sociological Society.

PAULA G. HARDWICK is currently working toward a master's degree in social work at the University of Oklahoma. Her interests are primarily in the achievement of the individual within diverse and fluid cultural contexts.

GEORGE HENDERSON is chairman of the Department of Human Relations at the University of Oklahoma. He is the author and coauthor of 20 books and more than 50 articles. His doctoral degree is in educational sociology from Wayne State University in Detroit. Dr. Henderson was appointed S. N Goldman Professor of Human Relations in 1969, and designed the university's master's degree curriculum for the Human Relations program. In 1985, he was named a David Ross Boyd Professor and in 1989, he was appointed to a third distinguished professorship.

SUSAN MARCUS-MENDOZA has a Ph.D. in Clinical/Community Psychology from Texas A & M University. She is an Assistant Professor of Human Relations and Women's Studies at the University of Oklahoma and a licensed psychologist.

DREAMA G. MOON is a doctoral student in the Department of Communication at Arizona State University. She is cofounder of the Project for Recidivism Research and Female Inmate Training and serves as co–principal investigator of the project. Ms. Moon's current research interests are the impact of the institutional structure on the interpersonal relationships of and among women prisoners and recidivism among female offenders.

KATHLEEN A. O'SHEA has a master's degree in Human Relations from the University of Oklahoma. As an ex-nun, she attributes her drive to fight oppression in all its forms to her years in Chile (1965–1973) during the Allende and Pinochet regimes.

GARRY L. ROLISON is Assistant Professor of Sociology at Arizona State University. He has published on topics that include African American class structure, the urban underclass, and African American student alienation. Dr. Rolison received his Ph.D. in Sociology from the University of California at Santa Cruz. He is a past National Science Foundation Minority Fellow, an American Sociological Association Minority Graduate Fellow, and a pre-Doctoral Fellow at the Center for Black Studies, University of California, Santa Barbara.

ELIZABETH SARGENT is a doctoral student in English at the University of Oklahoma, where she teaches writing. She developed an educational program for women in the Tulsa City/County Jail.

LYNDA DIXON SHAVER is a professor, researcher, and consultant in the areas of intercultural, health, and organizational communication. Dr. Shaver received her Ph.D. in Communication from the University of Oklahoma. A member of the Cherokee tribe, she began her health communication research with an organizational study of Indian Health Service in Oklahoma. Previously a teacher in both public schools and a junior college, she has been on faculty in the Department of Communication at the University of Oklahoma and the University of New Mexico in the Department of Communication and Journalism and the School of Medicine, and is currently at Indiana University at South Bend.

RUBY J. THOMPSON is an undergraduate student in the School of Social Work at the University of Oklahoma. Her current research interests are support systems for former prisoners and the impact of incarceration on the family, particularly mothers and their children. She was instrumental in developing the Children and Mother's Program (CAMP), and the Women's Resource Center, a support group for battered women. As an ex-offender and a recovering addict, Ms. Thompson understands the needs of the forgotten population of incarcerated women. As a Cherokee woman, she is familiar with how a population can become invisible in our society.

CHONG HO YU is a graduate student in Educational Psychology at the University of Oklahoma. He has a background in multimedia professions, including print visual media and computer programming. Yu wants to specialize in instructional media and international education and hopes to develop computer-aided instructional materials.